Commercial Complexes with Bionic Approach

Ava Hashempour

Title: Commercial Complexes with Bionic Approach
Author: Ava Hashempour
Cover designer: Ali Khiabanian
Publisher: American Academic Research, USA
ISBN: 9781947464247

Table of contents

Table of figures

Tables

Chapter 1:

Generalities of Study

Commercial and hotel complexes, and in general, a complex that is an active and dynamic complex in the form of a space defined within the city, can meet the needs of citizens in a desirable way. Since the commercial complexes are within the radius of the neighborhood of the complex, and wider in the urban and even metropolitan area, it will be a project with special service features.

One of the methods of sustainable development is the use of techniques adapted by nature. Contemporary man, in particular, is always striving to know and apply nature in order to know it. Conscious imitation in the current situation in the form of a case study of solutions in nature, means to achieve a database of successful solutions that will solve the problems facing humans today and its needs (especially in the field of architecture). We have always had as many resources to learn from nature and related systems as all available components. Bionic and naturalistic architects always have a new look at the structure. But on the other hand, the research approach in bionic architecture has characteristics that the most important principle in bionic architecture is that the building can show its vitality. Because engineers have long played a major role in the development of technology, activity in this sector should be carefully and thoughtfully guided so that it is in harmony with nature. Therefore, it would be appropriate to say that all ways of design end in nature (Rostami, Fatemeh, 2018). Nature around us needs inquisitive eyes and minds. Around us, there have always been many connections and communications in natural systems in a complete and safe way that engineers have used in the meantime. They are involved in the construction process and are always looking for the best methods in construction, which mainly increase quality and safety, reduce costs, save time and money. Therefore, in this process, bionics, materials science (metallurgy) and how to model and arrange materials from those systems will be introduced (Idem). Accordingly, the issue raised in this proposal is the design of a commercial complex that can represent the desired dynamics in the bionic modeled structure of the starfish.

So, in short, by carefully studying the starfish, we try to use its structure to design the roof of the bodies and organize the commercial complex. The structure according to which the specific approach of this proposal is suggested, is the focus on recognizing and analyzing the structure of the starfish in order to achieve the optimal bionic structure by simulating the shell and its other elements. Therefore, the main issue of research is understanding and applying the starfish concepts as well as utilizing them in the design of the proposed commercial complex architecture.

The use of modern methods derived from the structures of living organisms is an example of sustainable architecture. If we can achieve a kind of creative architecture with careful scientific scrutiny of starfish, it will be considered a new issue that firstly, less work has been done and secondly, a better understanding of the subject will pave the way for an optimal architectural design in terms of structure as well as hidden beauty in this living creature. The main purpose of this design includes to explain the architectural design solution of the commercial complex based on bionic structure and biophilic architecture.

Business Center which is also known as Shopping Mall or Shopping Plaza in English, it is a twentieth-century adaptation of the market, which has a long history. The mall is a collection of retail stores, service areas, and parking spaces for customers; all operated by a single management company, serve as a unit, is designed, built and operated. (Ibrahimi & Sadria, 2019). In addition to the above, business malls can have restaurants, banks, theaters, professional offices, service stations and other enterprises?

1.1 Definition of Bussiness Centers

Items that designers consider at the time of construction of the business center, including the facilities of the site in terms of demographic capabilities that can support such a center; full access for vehicles; dimensions, availability (Rahmati, Mahshid; Shoka Khoshbakht Bahrmani and Vahid Ghobadian, 2019); the topography of the site as well as the ability to use the welfare facilities of the zoning rules and land use in the surrounding areas. The economic conditions and sociology of the region, and local business competition as well as the way people perceive it, determine the size of a supported shopping center and the type of shop acceptable for a place. Business center are generally aimed at the people of the neighborhood or the inhabitants of an area or the population of a large geographical area. The smallest type of business center is the neighborhood one which has usually a supermarket in the center with shops like pharmacy, shoe store, and laundry. Such a center typically serves 2,500 to 40,000 customers within a 6-minute drive. The shopping center of the residents of an area includes all the above services, in addition to a department store which together with the supermarket form the center of the business center. Clothing stores, home appliances and repair shops can also be found in this type of shopping center. These types of centers offer services nearly 40,000 to 150,000 people. An area shopping center includes a full range of shops and stores that provide services similar to regional malls. This type of shopping center is built around at least one complete department store and often around several such stores. There are numerous specific stores and boutiques in these malls, and they usually have several restaurants and even a movie theater. Services related to daily needs are minimized. This shopping center covers a population of more than 150,000 or even 400,000 people or more. Larger motel sites, medical and health centers, or administrative buildings can also be built in these centers. Parking and car parking facilities are one of the major considerations in the design of any shopping center. The size and width of the shopping center, the type of tenant and the economy of the area partly determine the parking requirements. But today it is known that the ratio of 5.5 parking spaces per 1000 square feet (93 square meters) of rentable space is usually sufficient. The parking lot should be wide and easily accessible so that there is no traffic jam. On hill sites, it is often cost-effective to use the parking platform and related services separately from the main consumer classes. The movement of pedestrians and vehicles inside the center is one of the general design considerations and should be kept as spatially separate as possible. Exceptions to this rule are shops, theaters, and drive-in banks that are located on a satellite basis (relative to the mall). The first unified business center called Country Club Plaza, by GC. Nichols was founded in 1922 near Kansas City, Missouri, and the first enclosed mall opened in 1956 near Minneapolis, Minnesota.

(Figure 2.1) Country Club Plaza, Source, Maghsoodi, 2008

In the 1980s (megamalls) began to appear. For example, West Edmonton Mall opened in Alberta, Canada which encompassed not only 800 shops, but also everything from shoes to cars. It also includes several restaurants, a hotel, an amusement park, a miniature golf course, a church, a water park for sunbathing and surfing, a zoo, an artificial lake 133.5 meters and more than 500 different types of trees have been planted in the space of this megamall.

(Figure 2.2) Alberta Megamall, Source, Maghsoodi, 2008

1.2 Types of Shopping Center

Airport center: it includes retail, restaurants and other airport-focused services (Rahimi, 2011).

Arcade: it is a typical 19th-century public indoor shopping mall with an arched glass roof, and two rows of shops on either side of the pedestrian crossing are usually connected by two parallel streets.

Community center: a shopping center with an area of about 100,000-350000 square meters, which consists of one or two apartments, pharmacies and home appliance stores. These centers are roofless and built on the same floor with their shops in L or U shapes.

Convenience center: an open-air shopping mall with less than 6 shops that cater to the daily needs of people such as drinks, videos and other necessities.

Enclosed mall: a type of shopping center that is generally located within a roofed structure and is entered by a limited number of controlled entrances and the most shops are accessible through internal corridors.

Entertainment complex: a type of shopping center that includes places such as theaters, restaurants, and entertainment venues that are connected to retail stores.

Fashion mall: a shopping center consisting of shops that offer fashionable clothes and quality goods.

Festival market place: urban shopping malls that are a combination of restaurants and entertainment venues that are also associated with historical and cultural sites.

Galleria: a kind of glass-roofed or a courtyard shop like the Victorian European shops with glass vaulted ceilings. Like the Vittorio Emanuel Gallery, built in 1867 in Milan, Italy.

Life style center: an outdoor shopping mall that is lined up as outdoor shops, such as fashion, jewelry, and leather goods stores, as well as restaurants designed to attract wealthy consumers. These centers usually have attractive areas, fountains, seating areas that encourage customers to walk and shop.

Mall: large shopping malls (usually covered) with parking lots nearby.

Mix use center: a complex that may include residential homes, offices, restaurants, theaters, a hotel, and other uses associated with a retailer.

Neighborhood center: a shopping center that is not covered and has about 30,000-150000 square meters with 3 to 15 floors with a supermarket (Idem).

Open-air: a shopping center where shops are directly accessible to the public, its sidewalks may be covered, but these shops are not enclosed under a single roof.

Regional center: a shopping center with an area of 400,000 to 800,000 square meters, often covered with 40 to 100 shops.

Shopping center: a designed group of interconnected retailers, usually associated with a parking lot, often managed by an organization.

Strip: a small neighborhood shopping mall that is located outdoors and is usually smaller than 10,000 square meters with less than three rows of shops connected to the rows of parking lots in front of the shops.

Super-regional center: the largest type of shopping center that is classified according to requirements and usually an indoor space with an area of more than 800,000 square meters and more than 100 shops, which includes several chain stores.

Urban mall: an urban shopping mall, the largest of which may include several floors with access to multi-storey car parks.

Village center: a shopping center that is not covered and has several rows and often has a central square.

Value-oriented: a shopping mall marked by narrow auction shops.

1.3 The Evolution of the Design of Stores and Business Complexes in the World

1.3.1 History of Developments in Stores and Business Spaces

Buying and selling has always been an important part of human life. With the advent of agriculture, nomads became monogamous and established a more sustainable way of life, which led to the emergence of specialties and professions in society. In an agricultural society, the basic food needs of a society are met by a small percentage of the total population so that others can pursue other professions such as producing goods and providing services. Markets, often the commercial and social center of the city, made it possible for people to easily obtain the goods they needed by comparing similar goods, based on quality, quantity, and price. Such these factors that led to the competition between sellers and thus formed the basis of modern stores (Talebian, 2019). In fact, the business center (markets) is a collection of shops and related spaces that have existed in various forms since long time ago. It has continued up to now and has been the cause of progress and the beating heart of cities. Function of the Agora of the ancient Greece, which was originally devoted to religious ceremonies, and later to matters relating to the administration of the city, including the passing of laws and judgments, became something like the modern shopping malls built in the center of social and commercial activity of the city. The invention of money led to a revolution in the trading industry. Money provided the basis and unit for the supply of goods and services. Until now, people had to obtain the goods they needed via exchanging goods for goods with someone who needed their products. But with the help of money, goods are valued and can be easily bought and sold at any time and place.

1.3.2 18th and 19th Century Developments

During this period, markets and shops were moved from the open air to indoor environments, which changed the temporary nature of the market. Indoor markets such as the Milan Gallery made it easy to shop throughout the year, even in snow and rain (Bani, Masood, 2011, 187) and for the first time, they created the experience of leisure shopping and going to the market in their spare time. Initially, markets were limited to a specific commodity, but Deboa Gallery sold a variety of goods, unlike prototypes; as a consequence, different people and buyers were attracted to the market. After the French Revolution, these markets became a space for communication and meetings of different segments of the people of Paris. Balzac defines a mix of different types of people such as foreigners, nobles, poor people, gentlemen, vagrants, etc. in these markets who walk to shop, watch people and talk. In other words, these indoor spaces and arched markets have created a multi-purpose environment in the city center where social interactions were also addressed. As in the bookstores or cafés of the Americans at the Debua Gallery, Parisians took part in what he called a "passionate debate" in which they exchanged views and conversations quite freely. These political, social, or aesthetic debates owe to freedom that is nowhere to be found but here. The invention of price tags or etiquette created another revolution in the buying and selling industry. Previously, buying and selling required face-to-face communication between seller and buyer. The price tag enables buyers to search easily for the items they need and choose based on a predetermined price. Besides these factors, facilities and amenities also affected the sales industry in the late 19th century. Stores also offered more than one product, thus creating the experience of buying all the goods from one store and by combining different departments, it was possible to compare and purchase a variety of goods and services under one roof. As the market grew, so did the competition between idea vendors (customer service). John Van maker in Philadelphia and Marshall Field in Chicago save sales from chaos and disorder. Thus, the industry changed from mere customer acquisition to customer orientation (Idem).

Figure 3.2 Milan Gallery

1.3.3 Early 20th Century Developments. Source:
www.eavar.com

The modern department store industry was born in the early twentieth century with the mass production of cars by Henry Ford. During this period, cars were produced without regard to urban restrictions and routes and timetables, and provided easy and convenient transportation. But it soon became clear that the traditional structure of urban development was unable to meet the needs of traffic and parking for the increased number of cars. In Kansas City, a residential project contractor named GC. Nichols bought a swamp land due to the age of the car to build a commercial project in it and receive customers who will come there with their cars. In

1922, he established the Country Plaza Country Store, the first example of a suburban shopping mall. This complex, run by a private entity, gathered a set of shops and services in a single building and had free parking. In 1932, Hugh Perth opened the Highland Park Business Village on the Dallas suburb. The project was unique because it had an indoor car park located in the center of the building and surrounded by shops and stores.

1.3.4 1950s - The Generation of the Business Center Industry

Between 1950 and 1954, suburbs grew seven times faster than cities and permanently affected the American physical and social system. The current new society needed a new sales system, as a result of which a new sales industry and business centers were formed. Unlike the simple examples of the 1930s, the new shopping malls were a set of departments, stores, and personal rental units. In 1950, Northgate shopping malls were built in Seattle. This project, which was a perfect example of a shopping center, became a model for other shopping centers very soon. In 1954 J. L. Department Store of Hudson, Northland, opened in downtown Detroit, Michigan. The project includes 65,000 square meters of store space plus 55,000 square meters of Hudson store, which also includes Kruger grocery store and Keresgi furniture store. In 1956, Dayton Hudson South Dale built his property in Edina, a suburb of Minneapolis, Minnesota. The project, designed by Victor Grunn & Co., transformed the common design principles of shopping malls. And unlike the usual examples, which were a combination of a one-storey department store and covered hallways, South Dale Mall had two-storey department stores with rented shops. This indoor store had ventilation, heating and cooling facilities, and to ensure equal access to stores on both floors, the parking space was divided into two parts, half of which was used for the first and the other half for the second floor.

Figure 4.2 Business center. Source: *www.eavar.com*

1.3.5 1960s and 1970s - The Age of Growth and Influence

Migration to the suburbs made it possible to expand commercial centers without restriction. By 1960, shopping malls and stores were booming. The US economy had entered an incredible cycle of growth, and all economic and commercial activities had been successful. According to ICSC studies, 8420 shopping centers were built in 6 years, and after 2 years, this statistic reached 11580 units. In the 1960s, the Federal Legislature cancelled the Private Price Stabilization Act, which allowed manufacturers to keep their commodity prices at a maximum in traditional stores. The principle of consumerism and advertising was accompanied by the increasing growth of the countryside, and the development of stores continued in the 1960s and 1970s. The issue of advertising and global fame was raised among shopping malls and led to the expansion of this industry. The development of new cities continued in other cities and states and gradually, the new typology of shopping shifted the direction of the stores back to the city centers, in order to breathe new life into the city centers, which were now deserted and demolished. Following this, in 1962 Victor Grun designed the Midtown Plaza in Rochester, New York, which was immediately considered as a successful example of urban revitalization. The landmark project includes a number of administrative towers that connect to the city's central square with a large overpass, and a seven-storey office and multi-purpose commercial complex were later added. The process of reviving city centers continued with the construction of commercial projects, and different forms of business centers were created in different cities in accordance with urban areas. An example of this, is the Police Water Tower, which opened in Chicago in 1975 and was the first high-rise vertical shopping mall in the United States. This 74-storey multi-purpose complex was a combination of 8 commercial floors with a luxury hotel, administrative and residential units and parking. Police Water Tower turned Michigan Street into a world-class store space.

Figure 2.5 Police Water Tower Centers. Source:
http//firststateupdate.com

1.3.6 1980s until Now

Public transportation, globalization, and the Internet have made a huge difference in life, as well as in stores. People were saving a lot of money and there was a big change in the tourism, travel, sales and construction of special spaces and buildings. Consumers also became much more aware. Comparative shopping, customer survey reports, cheap shopping malls, department stores and now the internet have created increasing competition among sellers over price and quality. Executives of commercial projects turned to building chain stores. Thus, the number of traditional shops were reduced which mostly included rented spaces and shops. There were changes in the renovation of the main street of the city center and the traditional shop space. The government also agreed to provide more facilities and side spaces such as parking. In the 1990s, urban recreation centers grew globally. For example, the business and entertainment center of the people of Budapest, Hungary, is the Donna Plaza - A commercial and entertainment complex includes an indoor ice rink and 9 movie theaters. This is the first large passage to be built among the city's many shopping malls. Gradually, such complexes appeared on worn-out industrial sites in Europe and Asia. During this period, successful elements in the design of stores have been changing. Previously, if someone had 2 or 3 good and successful business center, they would still build another project if possible. While now speed of construction of commercial complexes has slowed down and the focus and emphasis of sellers and shop owners has shifted to attracting a new generation of consumers and greater productivity and profitability of existing real estate. During this period, the transportation and connection of urban and public spaces with private spaces became one of the main design issues. The use of private cars became common in most Third World countries. Traffic routes, public transportation, pollution, parking, etc. required new and better measures in the design of urban spaces. Especially in Europe, the technique of green buildings became a necessity for large projects and public investments. In Asia, environmental sustainability was considered to such an extent that in governmental and semi-government projects, the principles of sustainable architecture were required. In general, during this period, new theories related to technical issues and heat recovery, water control, solar energy systems, power generators and central ventilation and cooling systems were used in the design of large commercial projects around the world.

**Figure 2.6 New York Malls. Source:
http//:firststateupdate.com**

1.4 Bazaar

1.4.1 Bazaar Definition

A space in which goods are offered for sale or production and is a gathering place and often a communication route is called a bazaar. This is how Professor Harry defines Bazaar: A bazaar is a place where supply and demand intersect for a single price. The market is a geographical location that brings together a number of people whose trade leads to supply and demand and a unit price.

Figure 2.7 Tabriz mart. Source: lastsecond.ir

1.4.2 The Root of the Word Bazaar

The word bazaar, whose origin is next to "Vachar" and is still used as Vachar in Gilan and Natanz, is originally Persian and the word Bazargan is derived from it (Moin, 1993). The word entered the Portuguese language due to the Iranian trade with the Portuguese and from there to France and England, as they also call their Bazzar shopping center.

1.4.3 Bazaar Elements

During the formation of the market in different cities of Iran, several elements have emerged as their main and affiliated elements that the shape and form of each have been depending on the culture, climatic conditions, style of the time, and so on. Therefore, in order to fully and accurately identify these elements, we classify them based on the type of function and then describe each of them.

1.4.4 Spaces related to Warehousing and Storage of Goods

These spaces are one of the first architectural spaces that are important during the circulation of goods in the bazaar. Store or Kalanbar: It has been a place of storage and work on goods. Goods that are usually carried out by animals, should not enter the market. Hence, it was emptied through a parallel path called the back alley or behind the alley in the Khanbar (Pirnia, 2001, 123). The stores (Khanbar) were a large area behind the inn (Sara) where there were several small handicrafts and warehouses. Timchehs, inn, and caravansaries are each connected to the store separately.

1.4.5 Spaces related to Manufactured Goods

In bazaar, productive activities often existed in two ways: First, independent production activities that were carried out in industrial and similar workshops and second, the production activities that took place along with the sale of goods by small shops and workshops. Both of these activities are located in different architectural spaces as follows:

Dalan (corridor) … Gheisarieh … workshop

1.4.6 Spaces related to Commercial Activities

The main function of bazaar, which is the trade of buying and selling goods, took place in the spaces known as Pachal. In general, trading took place in well-defined and different spaces, each of which had a specific task of commercial activities. These places are: Chamber room (Hojreh Dokan) …. Caravansary (Sara) …. Timcheh … Khan …. Rasteh Bazar.

1.4.7 Spaces related to Service Activities

In each major and permanent market according to the size, extent and volume of trade in it, there were a number of service spaces such as reservoirs, stables or ostriches, snow pits, warehouses, bathhouses, stores, etc. such services were provided in this way. The number of such spaces and their position along bazaar depended on the physical and functional characteristics of. Large markets provided wide storage space for goods, while small markets with more retailers required fewer warehouses.

1.4.8 Spaces related to Public Activities

Due to the fact that the main and permanent bazaar of each city was the most important communication and public road of the city and the most commuting took place in it, many public spaces were built next to the main row of the bazaar and a short distance from it. For example, we can mention the Grand Mosque (Masjed Jame), which was usually built next to the bazaar, except in special cases. For this reason, in most of the historical cities of the country with its historical and ancient structure, the old texture of the city has not been completely changed in which the location of the Grand Mosque can still be seen in or between the city bazaars. Many religious schools and other administrative and public educational spaces such as Zurkhaneh and baths were built next to the bazaar.

1.4.9 Communication Spaces

Communication spaces in bazaar were presented in two ways: Spaces such as rows and alleys, spaces that existed only between two or more main spaces, such as indoor and short corridors where caravanserais connected mosques and other main spaces to the main row of the bazaar. In addition to the mentioned communication spaces, which were usually considered as part of the main spaces of bazaar, there were other more specific spaces that were mostly in charge of communication between other parts, such as Chaharsooq and Jelukhan.

1.4.10 Urban and Communication Elements and Spaces
- **The Main Row (Rasteh Asli)**

Since the main bazaars of Iran are often formed linearly and along the most important urban thoroughfares, the most important part and the main element of bazaar is its main row. A bazaar row was formed in its simplest form with shops located on either side of it.

Various guilds were stationed along a main line. In this way, each was placed in a part of the main row. In some large cities, two or more major rows arose in parallel or intersecting.

- **Sub Row**

Bazaars of very small towns had only one main row but in medium and large cities, in addition to the main row, a number of sub-rows appeared parallel or perpendicular to the main one.

- **Corridor (Dalan)**

Corridor is a communication space that often in architectural spaces and linearly acts as a link between the exterior and interior space of the building, or only between the interior spaces of the building. In large bazaars, corridor is a communication space and is often in the form of an alley or a small and sub-row that is related to one row to another and a caravansary to the other. There are usually a number of Chambers (Hojreh) and Stores (Sara) on either side of it. There are many corridors in Tehran Bazaar (Pirnia, 2001).

- **Semnan Bazaar Chaharsoo**

The intersection of the two main and important rows of the market is called Chaharsoo. In some cases, at the intersection of the two designed rows of the market, they often created a four-sided space that was considered valuable due to its communication position. Chaharsoo of Isfahan, Lar, Tehran, Kerman, and Bukhara Bazaar are good examples. In some historical periods, following the Arabic word "souq" meaning market, the word "chaharsooq" was used instead of chaharsoo.

- **Square**

Next to or along some of the major bazaars in large cities, there was an urban district square because the bazaar was the most important passage of the city and in most cases it was connected with an urban square. Isfahan Grand Bazaar are connected with two squares, Sabzeh Maidan (Old Square) and Imam Square (Naghsh Jahan). Ganjali Khan Square is located next to a part of Kerman Bazaar. Sabzeh Maidan is next to part of Tehran Bazaar and there is still a piece of its space. Sometimes there was one or more small squares along the bazaar, and in some cases in recent centuries, some of these were also called Tekiyeh or Hosseinieh. Some examples of such can still be seen in Semnan Bazaar as well as Tajrish Bazaar in Tehran.

- **Jelukhan**

Jalukhan, as an urban space, is a communication space in the form of a small square, which is surrounded on four or three sides and has a built-in space that was used as an entrance space, pause and gathering.

- **Elements and Spaces of Market Architecture**

The drapery room or the same shop of the drapery (shop) is the chamber or shop can be considered as the simplest and the smallest, but the most important element and space of bazaar. The area of chamber was very different and averaged from ten to twenty-five square meters. Chambers on the ground floor, level with the aisle, typically served as a shop, where goods were sold while the rooms on the upper floor of the two-storey bazaars were mostly used as the office and official space of a firm. Some of the rooms on the upper floors of the bazaars were also used as workshops.

Some of bazaar chambers were slightly (about fifty to seventy centimeters) above the level of the passage. In such form, in some cases, a warehouse was built under each chamber. Some of the rooms, in addition to the main space, had a part in the form of a safe house. It was located at the end of chamber, which was separated from the main space by a dividing wall.

Chamber is also the general name of the space that forms the caravansary. The rooms of the caravanserais were sometimes built on two floors, with chambers on the ground floor mostly having a commercial or workshop aspect, and the rooms on the upper floor often having an official and sometimes workshop aspect.

- **Caravansary (Sara)**

Caravanserais can be considered the most important architectural space designed in the markets and almost like today's passages. Maybe one of the reasons of appearing of caravanserais was the limited length of the bazaar rows, as today, if a commercial street is so prosperous that all the shops along it do not meet the needs of commercial spaces, gradually passages is built behind the shops and only their entrance is placed in the street, thus increasing the capacity of the commercial spaces of a street. In the past, if the main bazaar of a city was developed, a number of caravanserais would be built behind the main row and sometimes next to the sub-rows.

From the beginning of the present century, the word "Sara" has been gradually used in bazaar instead of the word "caravanserai". After the role of caravans in transportation was weakened and carriages, chariots, and then motor vehicles were used, the prefix "caravan" was removed from the word caravansary, and the urban caravanserai was called Sara. In the past, the word Sara meant house. The caravanserais were introverted spaces with a central courtyard with rooms on one or both sides on one or two floors.

- **Timcheh**

The word "Tim" meant a caravansary as Naser Khosrow has used this word in his travelogue. Timcheh meant a small Tim or a small caravansary. But in the contemporary period, caravanserais or small, covered inn are called Timcheh like Timcheh Amin al-Dawla in Kashan. This physical characteristic of the Timchehs means that they are covered, creating a suitable space for the supply of precious goods such as carpets, away from wind, rain and sun damage. Because of this, the Timcheh space is often more economically expensive than caravanserais and has not been used to supply cheap goods.

During the Qajar period, various designs of Timcheh and caravanserai emerged. Saracheh and Timcheh Amir in Tabriz and Sara and Timcheh Haj Reza in Qazvin are examples of this type of building.

- **Larestan Qaisaria**

The word Qaisaria is derived from the Latin word "Caesarea" meaning royal bazaar. In some sources it is mentioned that the word Caesarea was related to the word "Qaisar" or "Cesar". In Iran, the space was called Qaisaria, which in terms of architectural features was similar to a sub-row, Dalan or Timcheh and in a few cases similar to a Sara, but in terms of function was often dedicated to the supply of luxury and precious goods, especially excellent textiles. For this reason, the Caesarea space had one or more entrances, which were closed at night. There were examples of this type of Caesarea in Isfahan.

In some Ottoman bazaars in the historic cities of present-day Turkey, as well as in Syria and Algeria, there was a space called "Badstan" which some scholars have believed that its named derived from the Persian word "Bedeh Bestan (give and take)". Badstan function was quite similar to Caesarea one and was dedicated to the supply of precious goods, especially exquisite textiles.

Figure 2.8 Turkish Bazaar. Source: lastsecond.ir

1.5 History of the Islamic Bazaar

One of the features of Islamic culture that has not been widely used is the extraordinary migration and displacement of Muslims. Traveling in the deserts and arid lands, even today, discourages and worries Middle Eastern travelers. The religion of Islam emerged in a land that had centuries of experience in trade between Yemen and the Mediterranean. Islam was revealed to a man whose father was a businessman and who had traveled to Syria at least once with a caravan. From the first century AH onwards, Islamic armies conquered areas from the Pyrenees to the crossings of Central Asia and brought the caravans of the surrounding lands under the control of Dar al-Salam more than the military barracks and the rulers. The peaceful spread of Islam in the coastal areas of India, Southeast Asia and Africa was due to the opening of trade routes by merchants. Muslims had a great influence on trade and military relations by choosing suitable opportunities to build new cities (Ghobadian, 2016). In addition to the late commercial tradition, Islam evoked in Muslims another desire and reason to travel, and that was to perform the rituals of Hajj and pilgrimage to Mecca and other holy places of the Arabian Peninsula. In the teachings of Islam, commercial and religious activities were in no way separate. Hence, from the beginning, Muslims bought goods during the Hajj journey and paid for their journey by selling them. In the second century AH, pilgrimage to places in southern Iraq such as the holy shrine of Imam Ali and his sons Imam Hassan and Imam Hussein became popular, and in other Islamic regions, the tombs of the saints attracted Muslims. Therefore, in the Islamic lands, Muslims were constantly on the move for commercial, religious and educational reasons. During this period, with difficult road conditions, the city markets located in the heart of Islamic cities were the best shelter and safe place where water and food were abundantly available. Markets were also the most suitable centers for making all kinds of goods, especially small and exquisite utensils and goods that were difficult to manufacture and produced in the suburbs. Islam inherited a world where military equipment, trade routes, and commercial centers abounded, and all of them performed the same duties during the Islamic era before the establishment of Dar al-Salam. The use of Chapar houses and Chapar horses and couriers with houses between the two Chapar centers had been established for a long time during the time of Cyrus the Great Achaemenid. According to Herodotus, one of the inventions of the Iranians was to set up stations with magnificent guesthouses at various distances on the roads. The roads were always safe because there was always traffic. The number of houses or post offices on the Sardis-Shush road was 111. But there is no information about the architecture of these guest houses and it is likely that they were made of clay and brick, and because these materials have a short life, today nothing can be seen in the place of this building except a pile of soil. There is also scattered information about the road network and within 6 centuries from the time of Herodotus to the Roman period, silk entered the northern regions of Mesopotamia from China by land and by the Sassanid Empire and went to Rome. Or spices and perfumes were imported from India and Yemen via the western oases of Saudi Arabia and from there via the caravan cities of Batra (or Petra), Tadmor (or Palmura) and Dora - Europe to Rome - and later were transited to Constantinople. According to the writings of historians and geographers of the Islamic world, the bazaar, along with the Grand Mosque and the baths, were among the main elements of the Islamic city. Since Central Asia was more urban than the Mediterranean until the Achaemenid period, Soviet archaeologists proved that the buildings and functions were significant. However, pursuing their effects is still difficult. The architecture of the Islamic bazaar has three significant elements: A network of covered streets, roofed buildings and gates in the middle of it, and "Khan" which were equivalent to the caravanserai city. Every village and Islamic city with a bazaar usually had several baths. Market areas have been essentials. It is important to note that in all towns, there was a central bazaar with covered streets, a Khan, an entrance gate (which was closed at night) and a bathroom, all of which were gathered around the Grand Mosque. While in the big cities and state capitals there were a number of neighborhoods, in each of which these elements, like the central market, gathered in Chaharsooq parallel to the roads and the term Charsouq was a common concept in the markets of the Islamic world: The Arabic word souq means the covered streets of the bazaar, in other words, the bazaar; and the Turkish term Charsi was used to describe the entire market. In lands that were part of the ancient world and its remnants, bazaars were usually built around the Grand Mosque with the exact same arrangement. They had a function like the agora of the ancient world with surrounding buildings and porch streets. The distribution of trade goods was also significant: Containers and dishes were sold around the Grand Mosque; the suppliers of candles and frankincense were placed directly next to the mosque; they were accompanied by booksellers, stationery sellers, bookbinders, and scribes. The guild of merchants and clothing sellers also had their own markets but the market for fine fabrics and furs and other precious goods was separate. Various markets ranged from the home furniture market to the market for kitchen utensils and trivial items, to the suburbs and its gates and fortifications as well. The nearest market to the suburbs where the caravans gathered was tools and fitters and blacksmiths and other vendors and craftsmen who met the needs of the caravans. That is, Saddlers (Sarajan) who made saddles; fitters who sold stilts and other iron tools; sellers of sacks and ropes, tents and accessories that travelers on long journeys needed.

The furniture of the Islamic world, like the ancient world, was usually covered, and in general it can be said that their roof was composed of pounded soil, mud and wood, and their arches or domes were made of stone and brick. The complete market, which includes all these features, did not exist before the 15th century. There were usually bazaars where open space was covered with canvas canopies or tents, where food and daily necessities were sold. These types of markets were set up in certain locations and could be transferred to other places. Exceptions were the Horse Markets of Cairo and Aleppo. Separation of goods and their trade was also a feature of Islamic markets and originated in ancient times and was similar to Byzantine markets in the Middle Ages: Ibn Battuta visited Constantinople in the eighth century (AH) and reported that its markets were organized according to the goods in which they were sold. He also found that every market has gates will be closed at night. This was a characteristic of an Islamic bazaar and was usually called Caesarea. Caesarea was originally a covered rectangular porch with an arch and often a dome (as in the case of Ottoman Turkey), with a door in one or more directions that were closed at night for greater security. Its name was reminiscent of the covered market that Julius Caesar set up in Antioch, which the Byzantines called Caesarea. Market security was very important. The Ottoman emperors, known as the Bedouins, were like interior rooms located in the heart of the bazaars. In places like Burlington Arcade, London today, exquisite objects were traded: items such as Crimean stones, precious jewels and textiles, gold and silver were naturally linked to other financial activities such as coins, taxation and exchange. Thus, Caesarea was often considered the financial center of the government, where taxes and duties were collected, and funds were distributed to maintain municipal institutions. Of course, here it is not possible to compare this Caesarea with the Caesarea that Shah Abbas I, had set up in one of the terminals of Shah Square. In this building, royal caravanserais were located, with decorated attics that overlooked the square. It had shops selling fine silk textiles that were part of the government's economic planning. Warehouses were considered to be one of the most important elements of the Islamic market after the Souqs and Qaisariyya. The warehouse, which had various names and Khan was one of the most common, was basically a rectangular or square building with two or three floors with one entrance. Upper floors were attics with one-size-fits-all rooms with windows facing the market. But historical and regional factors had created a great variety in their roofing and other details. The merchants' rooms were on the upper floors, and the lower floor was dedicated to stables and large shops or warehouses for large goods; completion of Khans in a city of Islamic cities at a certain time; has shown happiness and abundance of blessings in that city. Today, in most Islamic cities, readers in the center of the bazaar are used for storage, and merchants do not use it for housing and production.

In general, based on above saying, can be concluded that:

- In the arrangement of Islamic markets, a kind of settlement hierarchy prevails. Surprisingly, this feature can be seen from North Africa to India. Food is usually sold outdoors, for example Risani in Morocco.

- The standard market plan includes a network of Sooq covered with arches, and tall domes and open, roofless space at intersections.

- The Central Asian market is usually surrounded by a wall, such as the recently built Bukhara Bazaar.

- The bazaar is one of the oldest features of the Islamic city and connects the commercial center of the city to the mosque, bath, khan and school. It is a miniature city that consists of several alleys and intersecting angles.

- Every material has a market for itself, such as the spice, leather, and blacksmith market.

- Each shop is a part of the market, and shopkeepers use the walls to display goods.

- Arched streets with openings in the center of each which provide a cool and gentle atmosphere in hot weather.

Figure 2.9 Tehran Bazaar

1.6 Bazaar in Iran

1.6.1 Overview of the Trend of Historical Development

The phenomenon of Bazaar in Iran has maintained its continuity throughout history from the beginning of the emergence of human societies. By studying its historical evolution, we can determine what important events and the passage of time have affected it. In the early settlements of Iran, whose economy relied on handicrafts and commerce, there were probably places for industrial, commercial, and trade use that were somewhat close to the concept of the market. However, due to the economic structure of the country and the function of cities, except for port cities, in other cities, the market has been an important factor in the trade and production of some goods throughout the year. In the Sassanid period, due to the prevalence of domestic trade and the development of cities and urbanization, such an atmosphere emerged. In most of the big cities, including ancient Seleucia and Ctesiphon, large markets were formed where various goods (metal products, textiles, cereals and fruits) were produced and sold. Initially, the bazaar was formed outside the gates of Sharestan in the vicinity of Rabd and in a very basic way, and with the subsequent expansion, with the importance of trade and commerce, it was entered into the city so that in the city of the Sassanid period, the element of the bazaar in the backbone of the city started from the heart of civilization and expanded its scope to Rabd and became the heart of the city. With the establishment of Muslim rulers, and due to the existence of trade regulations and laws derived from Sharia and finally relative security in the country, trade flourished more than ever. Given the existence of such examples of markets in pre-Islamic cities, this element also played a key role in organizing the city of the Islamic period. And the most important policy of the Islamic government, which is to emphasize the importance of rabbis as a place of residence for craftsmen and professionals, as opposed to Sharestan as a place of residence for the privileged classes of society, caused the markets to be dragged from Sharestan to Rabz due to the transfer of centers of activity and in this part, become more important and broader. According to the tradition left over from the cities of the Sassanid period, the bazaar was pulled from the main square of the city to the wall and then expanded beyond it to a reasonable extent. With the creation of the Grand Mosque, there was an important change in the structure of the bazaar and the regulation of its space. The Grand Mosque became part of the city system, and the bazaar gained a special place as a center of business for the people, and was often located next to the Grand Mosque. Accordingly, the market spaces were planned and located. With the development of cities, the number of emerging markets also increased. Islamic cities have been woven around bazaars in their evolution and have created new markets in their expansion. It is on this basis that the bazaar can be mentioned as the backbone of the city of the Islamic period. In this evolutionary process, with the rapid development of trade and industrial production in the late second and early third centuries (AH) with the rise of governments and the Islamic state, scientific and technical exchanges took place in a wide area of the world at that time along with trade and commerce. Markets full of goods and people in these cities showed the economic power of the city of the Islamic period. This trend was interrupted by the Mongol invasion in the seventh century. After the Mongol period, due to the richness of the concept of the market in the urban system of Iran, with the effort to rebuild, which began in every part of the country, urbanization began to grow slowly and with the establishment of the Safavid state as the most centralized Iranian state in the Islamic period reached its peak again. The security created during this period and the development of Iran's foreign relations led to the expansion of foreign trade and, as a result, the prosperity of the production of various products. As the prosperity of the bazaars increased to meet the needs of the people, the inn, Timcheh, and Qaisariyyah came to work one by one, inevitably settled along with the specific texture of the bazaar, public places such as baths, schools and mosques, Imamzadeh, Takiyeh, Saqakhaneh, Zurkhaneh, coffee house, etc. were also placed next to it. All in all, a complete and unified context was created. Perhaps this period can be considered as the period of conceptual and physical evolution of the Iranian market (Habibi, 2019).

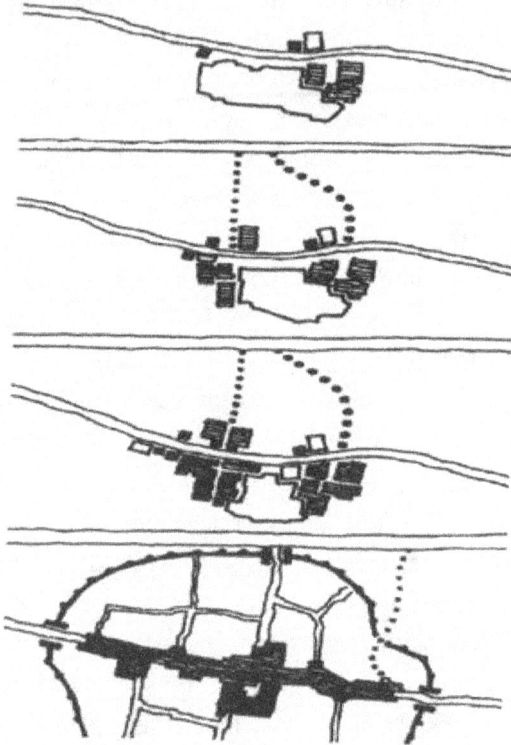

the trend of physical development of both, city and bazaar

Figure 2.11 the trend of physical development of both, city and bazaar. Source: Habibi, 2019

Figure 2.13 Kashan Bazaar. Source: www.snapptrip.com

1.7 Types of Markets

1. Rural Markets: it is formed more periodically and in connection with a number of neighboring villages and in proportion to their production on an annual, monthly, weekly, etc. The role of the rural market is similar to the urban market in many ways and in the villages of Iran, in addition to the economic aspect, it also has a cultural and social role. Such as meeting people, exchanging news and information, choosing a spouse, recreation, holding competitions, celebrating important historical events, resolving disputes and collecting taxes have all been done in them. There are weekly markets in densely populated rural communities such as the southern shores of the Caspian Sea and parts of Azerbaijan, and in a way it meets the needs of the scattered population of those areas which, due to the favorable climate, has abundant agriculture and crops. In the central arid plateau of Iran in remote units with small populations, such markets are either very rare or non-existent. In these areas, larger or main parts of smaller areas are divided. Commercial and industrial activities take place in the markets of the main centers.

2. Nomadic Markets: These markets are also often seasonal and for the exchange of nomadic livestock and handicrafts produced in certain seasons. These markets form a complete network in connection with rural markets as well as urban markets.

3. Urban Market: Markets that are formed in cities or their areas and have different forms and meanings according to their function, which are as follows:

a) City Market: In the cultural aspect of Iran, the city market is considered as the central part of trade. City is a political, commercial, cultural and religious center, and the market plays an important role in achieving this. Most cities in Iran have a main market.

b) Regional Market: In large cities, in addition to the main market of the city, there was one or more regional markets that met some of the needs of the residents of the area for daily, weekly and sometimes monthly goods. The functional area of these markets included a range consisting of two or more neighborhoods, and in some of them special goods were offered.

c) Neighborhood Markets: These bazaars provide the simple and daily needs of the locals, including food and other essential goods. It is usually supplied from a central market.

d) Suburban Markets: These markets are located on suburbs and often in the form of linear markets along the roads branching off the city gates and are the junction of the city to the village and are often for cheap goods like the southwest gate market in Shiraz.

e) Pilgrimage Market: In these markets, which are usually located in the neighborhood of holy places and Islamic shrines, most of the goods of places of pilgrimage are sold, such as candles, seals, rosaries and so on.

Figure 2.14 Tehran Bazaar

1.8 Conceptual Evolution and Market Structure in the Contemporary Period

The evolution of Iranian markets is due to various historical, social, economic, political, technical and other factors and phenomena, especially the monopolization of Iran's economy based on oil extraction and sale and the emergence of capitalism dependent on urban exogenous growth. The important change in the concept of the market and the change in the direction of a trend that went on for almost hundreds of years, took place during the Qajar period and with the change of life on a global scale. And with the changes resulting from the new economic system and the new way of life, the position of the markets in the urban life changed. The lack of a proper court organization and the authoritarian rule of the

Qajar princes practically destroyed the country's production organization and caused foreign capital to invade the country's economic and production organization. This caused the country to lose self-reliance of many consumer goods and the transformation of the consumer society began. Under these circumstances, the integration and integration of Iran's economy in the world market in the new conditions of the industrial economy, practically led to the disintegration of small and local markets. And commercial spaces are scattered and concentrated along the streets and throughout the city. Markets often became old and historic spaces. As a result of these developments, the markets of Iranian cities have faced different destinies:

1. Some of them are worn out due to isolation and loss of access and gradually they moved to the sidewalks. Erosion of empty spaces caused their destruction (Semnan Market).

2. Another group fragmented the streets, and the remaining sections undertook different activities depending on the new location in the city (Ardabil Market).

3. Some markets have retained their original identity due to the richness of the region in the production of domestic industries (Isfehan Bazaar).

4. In big cities, especially in Tehran, bazaars, in addition to some of their functions, have also started new activities. In these markets, the location of ancillary services, warehousing and supply of some goods, even in the worn parts of the market has caused a significant boom.

5. The widening around the holy shrine of Imam Reza has almost destroyed the old bazaar of Mashhad except for

a small row of Sarshur and a few other humble rows, almost nothing is left. Historic buildings around the shrine of Hazrat Masoumeh in the religious city of Qom and the shrine of Hazrat Abdul Azim in the city have also been destroyed. Qaisaria Bazaar of Shushtar with its beautiful square and cross-shaped plan has been destroyed due to street construction. Traditional Iranian markets were the center of collective life. To meet the general needs, the market has a number of buildings with a suitable design and location to accommodate various activities.

The structural elements of the big market of the city are in the most complete physical form and with the most extensive functional area as follows:

1. Spaces related to maintenance and warehousing: Sara, caravanserai and store (Khanbar)
2. Long spaces with corridor or band: Caesarea, workshop and shop
3. Commercial spaces: Dokan, Timcheh, Tim, Khan, Rasteh
4. Spaces related to religious and cultural functions: mosque, Hosseinieh, Tekyeh, Scientific Schools.
5. Spaces related to service functions: bathroom and water storage
6. Spaces related to social and communication functions: Zurkhaneh, Naqarkhaneh, Charsooq, Meidan, Jelukhan and caravanserais out of the city.

1.8.1 Tabriz Bazaars
Chardin, a French tourist, writes about Tabriz in the late Safavid era: "Tabriz is the first city of the country in trade". He mentions the population of the city in the 11th century AH

as at least 600,000 people and tells about the city: "Its mansion is not great, but its markets are more prosperous than other cities and their roofs are higher. The movement of people in this market and the abundance of merchandise is the reason for the development of the city."

plan of Tabriz Bazaar in the Qajar period

Figure 1.15 Tabriz Bazaar. Source: Habibi

1.8.1.1 Physical Characteristics

Tabriz Bazaar is one of the largest traditional markets in Iran and the world. This market has not only expanded linearly, but has expanded in the four related directions by forming several main and sub-rows. This is a multi-axis market. The area of Tabriz Bazaar leads from the north to Sahib Al-Amr complex, from the south of Bam to Alishahi Mosque or

Citadel, from the east to Kaboud Square and from the west to the Grand Mosque in a row. Tabriz Bazaar Economic Complex has a total area of 13 hectares, of which about 7.2 hectares are dedicated to the commercial sector only. Tabriz Bazaar is a communication network consisting of a number of parallel and intersecting rows. Its two main rows are the North-South row which are naturally parallel to each other. There are a number of rows perpendicular to these two rows, the most important of which are the route and extension of Haram Khaneh, Kafashan, and Meschi Bazaar. In this market, each of the coherent rows or spaces is dedicated to the supply of special goods and is also called by that name. The crossing of Aji Chai River from the north of the bazaar separates the context of the bazaar from Sahib Al-Amr Square located in the north of the river. In order to solve this problem, the market line has been extended from the foot and has established the connection between the market space and the square. This physical form is unique in its kind and there is no similar example in any other market. Tabriz Bazaar due to cold climate and extensive trade; has a dense, compact, and _covered (dorost)_ context. Most of the physical spaces of the bazaar are two and sometimes three-storey. The ceiling height of the rows is low - Maximum 6 meters - the width of the rows is between 4 and 5 meters. The roof of the long rows of the market with its maze and the combination of unique atmosphere, has caused a kind of thermal moderation, which creates warm winters and cool summers in the market space. The economic and commercial function of Tabriz Bazaar has been more than its socio-cultural function and it is perfectly seen in the combination of market elements. Mosques are also scattered around the commercial fabric. The concentration of mosques was mainly seen next to the Grand Mosque in the southwest of the bazaar. Baths are also less common in the central part of the market and are often located in residential alleys that end to the market area.

Figure 2.16 Tabriz Bazaare

Figure 2.17 Tabriz Bazaar

1.8.2 Isfahan Markets

Isfahan has been one of the great and famous cities of Iran throughout history. The city is located at the intersection of major and important roads; during the Achaemenid period, they were of special importance and were located on the way to Persepolis and Ekbatan. In the early Islamic period, the main elements of the city were located on the main axis or backbone of the city. This axis is probably from the branches of the Silk Road or part of the Spice Road (Rahe Advieh).

1.8.2.1 Physical Characteristics

The development of Isfahan complex can be divided into two old parts with a linear organization that was built over time and a new part that was built in a shorter time and with a better networked and orderly organization. This bazaar starts linearly in front of the Grand Mosque and the Old Square of Isfahan and expands in the north of Naghsh Jahan Square as a network and finally covers the entire square. In this complex, Qaisaria Bazaar, as the most beautiful and important row of Isfahan Bazaar, by the order of Shah Abbas, is located in the main axis of Naghsh Jahan Square, along with other physical elements such as Shah Caravanserai, Mint and Charsouq, which are very similar to Lar Bazaar. The role of Charsouq in the market of Isfahan can be seen in two ways: one in the collision of two market orders such as Charsouq Chit Saz, Charsouq Karbas Sales and Goldsmiths, as well as Charsouq Ashraf Gate; another is the existence of a valuable physical space next to the main row and the creation of a space pause such as Charsouq Qaisaria, Saroutaghi, and Mokhles. Except for Qaisaria Bazaar, which is the widest part of Isfahan Bazaar, other bazaars such as Dar Al-Shfa, Darbagh, Nimavar, and Mokhles Bazaar with a supply of about 5 meters and a height of about 10 meters have a width to height ratio of about one to two.

Inn (Sara)

One of the features of Isfahan Bazaar is its numerous inns. In the manuscript that has survived from the late Safavid era and is kept in the British Museum, 43 caravanserais and bazaars in Isfahan are listed, but unfortunately only a handful of them are remained. Most bazaars are two-storey and have porches across the second floor overlooking the courtyard. Sarai Shah, as one of the most important bazaars, was built by the order of Shah Abbas Safavid with about 160 rooms in two-storey. Important bazaar Sara are:

Mokhles, Haj Karim, and Golshan Sara

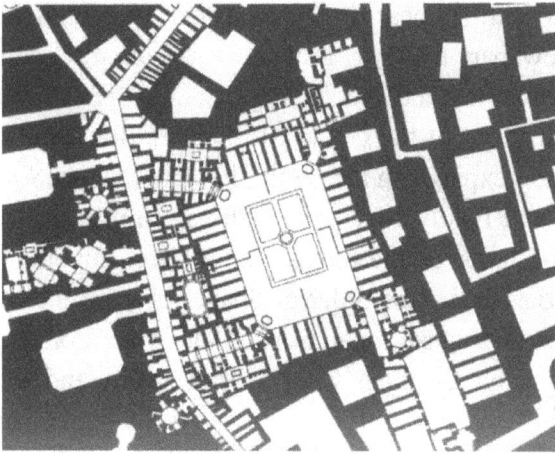

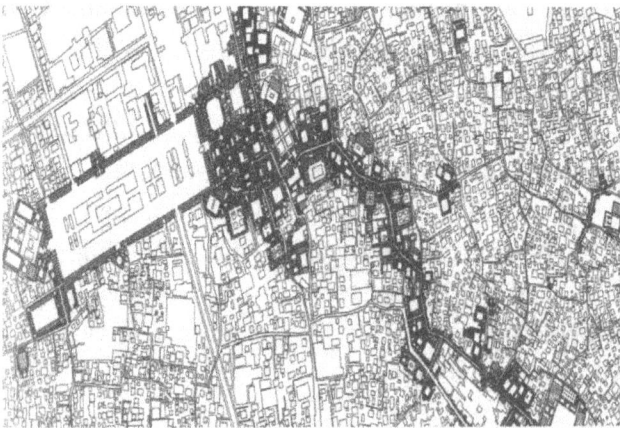

Figure 2.18 Isfahan Bazaar. Source: Pirnia

Isfahan Bazaar plan and surrounding residential context Timcheh

There are several Timchehs in Isfahan Bazaar, each of which has special physical characteristics in accordance with its functional characteristics. Among them, we can mention three Poosti, Malek and Jahangiri. These spaces are one of the most beautiful parts of Isfahan market.

1.8.3 Kerman Bazaar

The formation of Kerman Bazaar was on the north-south road of Khorasan, which passed through the west of the city. Later, new neighborhoods grew along the bazaar, facing north, and continued until the 7th century (AH). In the 8th century, with the expansion of the city, the bazaar shifted to the east and the east-west row of the bazaar began to grow. In the 11th century, coinciding with the Safavid rule and the economic prosperity of Kerman, the Ganjali Khan complex was built in the center of the city and at the intersection of the old bazaar axis and the new east-west axis. The location of this complex next to the old bazaar, ie the north-south bazaar, and at the intersection of the east-west bazaar, shows the gradual importance of the east-west bazaar. Of course, it is not correct to think that the formation of the East-West market coincided with the construction of the Ganjali Khan complex because when it comes to buying people's houses to build this complex, the name of the bazaar is taken to form an optional part of the east-west bazaar that was built before this period. But so far it has been less important than the north-south market.

1.8.3.1 Physical Characteristics

Kerman Bazaar includes a combination of organic markets and markets created by rulers or merchants at different times.

This combination has created an integrated complex leading to the city gates. Some of these complexes, such as Qala-e-Mahmoud Bazaar, are a thousand years old; others, such as the Mozaffari Bazaar and the Grand Mosque, the beautiful Ganjali Khan complex, and many other spaces, have been built in recent centuries. This complex along with several other ones (such as Ebrahim Khan, Vakil, Sardar, Haj Agha Ali) from the Qajar period along with elements such as bazaars, inns, etc. have created one of the most beautiful markets in Iran. In general, today's bazaar of Kerman, after different periods of its development, is an east-west bazaar that starts from the Mozaffari Grand Mosque and ends at Arg Square. The main part of the North-South Bazaar row is the part of the bazaar that starts from Rigabad Gate and extends to the end of the Shoemakers Bazaar. These two rows of bazaars intersect in Charsouq Ganjali Khan. This Charsouq is the common chapter of the two important markets of the city and an important point in the Kerman market. East-West Bazaar, which is located on both sides, the gate of the Arg and the Grand Mosque, divides the city into two parts, north and south, with a length of about one kilometer. The oldest part of this bazaar, which starts in front of the Grand Mosque, is known as Mozaffari Bazaar. With the construction of buildings on both sides of this bazaar, the "square" became the "row of the bazaar". After Mozaffari Bazaar, to the west Vakil, Ekhtiari, Ganjali Khan, Seraji and Naqarkhaneh markets, are loated respectively. Most of these markets have been built along this communicative-connective East-West axis between the two gates and two important nuclei of the city, namely the Grand Mosque and the Government Arg, and in different historical periods from the Safavid period onwards. In fact, this extension has been built in different historical periods from the Safavid period onwards due to the existence of two important nuclei of the city, namely the Grand Mosque and the Government Arg. Indeed, this extension has been formed due to the existence of two important urban nuclei on both sides since pre-Safavid times and in competition with the North-South row. With the emphasis on the urban and regional role of Kerman Bazaar in contrast to its commercial and trade role, the old bazaar row has gradually transferred its role to this direction. This part of Kerman market includes the following markets and complexes from west to east, respectively.

1. Nagharkhaneh Market
2. Seraji market
3. Charsouq Caravansary
4. Ganjali Khan Bazaar Complex
5. Ekhtiari Bazaar
6. Bazaar Vakil Complex
7. Mozaffari Bazaar Complex
8. Grand Mosque (Masjed Jame)

North-South market and its elements: The North-South Bazaar, which was in fact the primary market of Kerman and was located along the Silk-Spice trade route; nowadays, has largely lost its generality and continuity. By transferring the most of its role toward the East-West row, its properity will diminish.

North Row:
1. Aziz Bazaar
2. Haj Agha Ali Bazaar and complex
3. Row of shoemakers' bazaar
4. Kolah Mali Bazaar (Khajeh Momeni)
5. Ibrahim Khan bazaar and complex

South Row:
1. Castle Square Bazaar
2. Ghaleh Mahmood Bazaar

Figure 2.19 Ganj Ali Khan

1.9 Types of Business Complexes and their Constituent Parts

- Temporary markets (temporal and spatial)
- Permanent markets (day markets - general markets)

The general markets themselves include the administrative, sales and service sectors, each of which includes the following elements and has been studied separately.

1. Administrative Department: This section included companies and trading houses that were located and distributed in different parts of the market in the form of chamber.

2. Sales Department: This section consists of the following four sections, which are divided according to the type and amount of sales:

a) Partial sales:

It included handicrafts and shops, and grocereries, and so on.

b) Retail sales: (more than total sales)

This section includes specialized markets such as goldsmiths, shoemakers, etc.

c) Total sales: (more than retail sales)

In the form of collaborating masses or usually in this way.

d) Total sales:

In this section, sales by ordering and delivery of goods were done directly in warehouses.

Architects have long been inspired by nature. In ancient times, the columns of temples and palaces were made in imitation of palm trees or lotus flowers and the designers of the buildings have also used natural shapes and proportions in different cases to achieve aesthetic and eye-catching patterns. Today, some architects believe that imitating nature will be far more beneficial than beautifying the appearance of buildings. Therefore, they try hard to copy the structural rules of nature. For example, they use natural patterns to cool the living environment, generate energy, and even desalinate seawater. They emphasize the use of nature-based designs and natural patterns, not just a flamboyant slogan that is a vital but it economically and financially is a cost-effective issue. Architects and designers believe that nature-inspired designs can help reduce environmental damage (Hagan, S: 2001). Bionic design is a method that concerns the architecture of the building by inspiring the nature. According to the objectives of the present study, the theoretical foundations related to bionic architecture will be discussed in this chapter. For this purpose, the characteristics, history, and various methods of this type of architecture will be studied. Due to the study of executive projects with the desired approach, examples are another part of the study of this chapter. In the following, the issue of the airport and the development of the terminal of Imam Airport will be discussed.

1.10 The Concept of Nature

The natural environment is a set of biological and non-biological factors (physical, chemical) that affect the life of an individual or vice versa. Today, this definition is often related to man and his activities, and the environment can be summarized as a set of natural factors of the earth, such as air, water, atmosphere, rock, plants, etc. that surround man. The difference between the environment and nature is that the definition of nature includes a set of natural, biological and non-biological factors that are considered exclusively while the term environment has been described in terms of the interactions between man and nature and from his point of view (Karami, 2011). Nature is the first context of human life and other creatures. The coexistence of nature is directly related to the survival of human beings. In the following, the relations between man and nature are examined.

1.10.1 Relationships between Man and Nature

More than 2,000 years ago, Plato concluded that the most difficult human task in the world is self-knowledge. This fact must be constantly explored as many of its implications are not yet fully understood (Hall, 2008: 220). In 400 BC, the ancient Greek philosopher Hippocrates stated that we learn many things by imitating animals. We are the young disciples of the spider, we imitate it in weaving and making clothes, we learn how to build houses from swallows, we learn how to sing from swans and warblers (Senoozian, 2010: 12). There are many benefits to imitating nature. Suppose every living thing is the product of millions-year evolution. In the meantime, nature has destroyed everything that is not compatible with its specific purpose, giving rise to the hope that human beings, by studying the process of evolution, will copy the new mechanisms of technology from living things.

During 38 billion years of creation; Earth and Nature have been their ultimate designer and architect. During this time, plants and animals were able to overcome environmental problems with the necessary design (Mahmoodi Nejad, 2009). The French philosopher Jean-Jacques Rousseau stated that when our values disappear, we tend to return to the nature. The nature has all the answers and it is humans who are gradually learning how to get answers from nature. Because the "Book of Nature" can not be interpreted at first glance. Famous architects, engineers, and scientists strive to convey its message. In nature, there is a wide range of natural phenomena, such as the bodies of lizards or frogs, spiders, the flight of a bird, how insects function, or the design and behavior of a fish in water. They observe the principles of animal, plant, and mineral climates to apply them in human life to improve it. Following this discussion, the introduction of bionic science seems necessary because bionic science is interested in creating functions and shapes comparable to the functions and shapes of living organs. This is possible through observation, research, analysis and synthesis. This science is based on the hypothesis that any model can potentially provide ideas for the design of mechanical methods and components that will lead to the improvement of existing cases. Bionic science not only studies the physical and chemical aspects of a natural model, but also examines its structures to apply them to the structure of artificial tools and systems that are later used by humans (Senoozian, 2010: 10).

In the esoteric harmony of bionics and nature, it is enough that if an organism, for example, a bear, succeeds in different places and climatic conditions, from Asia and the Americas to the North Pole, is able to adapt not only to its diet but also to its physical structure and even skin color; why an architectural work can not achieve such compatibility (Mahmoodi Nejad, 2009). The effect of environmentally friendly architecture can be longer and create more well-being. Due to the relationship between man and the natural environment, nature has always been the source of human inspiration.

1.10.2 Nature is the Source of Human Inspiration

Every invention born of human thought, even only for human use, subconsciously approaches the infinite source of genius and the power of nature. Unfortunately, today's architectural values with a consumerist approach to construction, conventional forms and with personal preoccupations and regardless of the environment, have forgotten the diverse range of natural forms. The form and function of nature architecture is a process that we understand instinctively and internally as the evolution of growth and creation. Its most basic level is the commitment to life, which manifests itself in the form of interests. Architecture gives form and shape to the invisible beat and rhythm of life, and is in fact a flow that gives structure to design and vice versa. Architecture is a process that organizes and combines the various related forces into the overall shape of a unit. The components of a whole may seem unbalanced, but they will never appear unrelated. The more we become acquainted with its depth and evolutionary power. Every living organism is driven by an unchangeable force. It strives to make form and performance as efficient as possible. In the natural realm, it is very important to define "performance" as a process and relationship and "form" as the result of that process. Form is shaped by interaction with nature, and function naturally moves in the direction of adapting its relationship to the wider environment and its surroundings. Of all the creatures, humans seem to have the least innate talent for intelligent design. We can only learn, and to this end the open book of nature is the best source of learning for us.

What remains unknown is the answer to the question of how living organisms such as termites, bees, larvae, otters, and thousands of other species have such in-depth knowledge of how to build structures with such imagination, precision, and technical skill (Cook, 1996). The most important thing here is to understand the power of nature design for its practical use in human architecture. In searching for the missing link between nature and architecture, it seems necessary to study the processes of simulation and replication in nature and architecture. The shape of the human body, its uniqueness, and its identity composed of distinct parts; have taught man the first law of composition: Unity while multiplicity and diversity. Whether the human body is conscious in design or not, it is an essential part of all architectural civilizations, regardless of their period and time. The use of animal body features in a large number of human civilizations has enabled architects to use symbolic imitation to make connections between their ideas and to create the values of society. Characteristic traits of each animal and each of its body parts (wings, claws, beak, horns and skin) such as tiger skin have been used in the construction of buildings to achieve magical powers.

The praise of the mountains as landmarks of the world inspires the irresistible human desire to build symbolic mountains such as ziggurats, pyramids, and temples, as well as the skyscrapers and structures of residential buildings that follow the landscape around them today (Sadeghi, 2007). Man imitates nature in different ways. The following are the types of attitudes towards nature.

1.10.3 A Variety of Attitudes towards Nature

The influence of nature on architecture is different in each school; therefore, the principled analysis of the data of the body seems incomplete to understand the theoretical foundations of different schools in relation to nature. There are generally three main attitudes towards nature:

- Functional attitude towards nature;
- Philosophical view of nature;
- Religious and mystical attitudes towards nature.

Due to the nature of the research, it is enough to introduce a few views of theorists and architects in this field.

According to Boulding, the most important point in the classification of nature is the evolution of natural structures from non-living to living. Being alive in architecture means a two-way interaction between man and the nature around them (Sharghi & Ghanbaran, 2008: 108).

Some researchers, such as Boulding, see the world as a super-system consisting of many systems with different hierarchies and levels. His ranking was based on the differences in the rules governing the types of systems and their heterogeneity. The nine-tier system introduced by Boulding on this basis starts from solids at the lowest level and leads to cultural and symbolic systems (Mahmoodi Nejad, 2007: 10).

Table 1.2 Boulding table with a new attitude (Kish, Durrani and Mir Sharghi 2014)

Examples	Explanation	Rank and system level	
Atom, molecule, crystals	Fixed set	Static system	(inanimate
Clock, ordinary machines, solar system	Fixed-trend moving set	Mobile system	
Controllable machines, computers	Variable mobile set	Controllable mobile system	Mechanism system)
Chemical, digestive, gene and cell changes	Mobile complex with inherent changes	Transformable system	
Plant cells, leaf flowers	Live set with spontaneous growth, reproduction and division	plant	
Birds, insects, fish	Complete communication between learners and recipients and initiate awareness	Animal	Organism (living system)
Man	Complete intelligence and communication, symbolism, self-awareness of the future and past of the world	Man	
Family, community, customs, and trade	Expansion of human relations, laws, traditions, and language	Public culture of the community	Meta-organism (intelligent
Moral values, religion	Quality excellence in human thought and insight	Transcendent and symbolic thought	

According to Wright, all man-made objects enjoy life, and that is where its beauty lies. In their construction, love is used and this love comes to life with objects and proves or denies the quality of the civilization of the builders (Sharghi & Ghanbaran, 2008: 108). From the beginning, they blended their home with nature, but it was so elaborate that it was difficult to discern where nature ends and where their building begins. Wright tried to keep nature pristine (Mahmoodi Nejad, 2009: 397).

According to Charles Jackson, systems of nature go beyond predictable systems and are indeed unpredictable. Architecture must also be the result of man's view of himself and the world around him and today's conditions, in terms of science, technology and philosophy. According to modern science, the world today is a combination of order and disorder. The nonlinear, concave, and curvilinear architecture that is developing and evolving today is influenced by today's physics perspectives that identify the universe with waves and elements of particles. But David Pearson has the opposite view of Jackson: "Their work (architects like Jackson) conflicts with their beliefs; because these fragmented forms, full of sharp angles, displaced shapes, and advanced synthetic materials, all cast doubt; not organic integration and design to be able to elevate architectural works to something more than a sculptural work (Kish, Durrani and Mir Sharghi, 2014)".

Fractal theorists, in order to simplify the modeling of the geometry of nature, made the method of work as a principle, and it is a homogeneous repetition from part to whole. In this theory, originality is with part. In such a way that the whole is a function of it, but not an objective function, but a random and unpredictable function (Sharghi & Ghanbaran, 2008, 108).

According to Tadao Ando, creation of building is as a part of nature. He used architectural volumes as trees, rocks and mountains, and in the process of his creations he sought to recreate the taste of nature (Mahmoodi Nejad, 2009, 397).

Le Corbusier had a new look at nature. By designing Villa Sava in Poissy, France, creating a large terrace and placing empty frames in its facade, he created a mediator between interior architecture and outdoor nature. He wanted to drag the nature into the architecture (Mahmoodi Nejad, 2009, 398).

According to Paul Koleh, just as children imitate adults in their play, we must imitate the forces that made the world.

According to René Descartes: Celestial and terrestrial bodies are of the same genus and are components of a whole.

1.10.4 Strategies for Dealing with Nature

Natural phenomena are divided into three major categories: inanimate objects, plants, and animals. In order to create in general and design in particular, the most important and abundant existential principles (design) governing these phenomena can be used as a pattern. An examination of the above three categories and some of the natural principles governing their existence follows:

1.10.4.1 Inanimate Natural Structures

Natural forces that give rise to the formation and deformation of natural building forms are either derived from the manifestations of the Earth or have a general aspect. The building forms in the Earth's solid crust are generally the product of the effects of these forces. Earth folds have different shapes depending on the root and the effect of the forces. A non-living natural form, in addition to being formed under the influence of external forces, also tries to have maximum efficiency with the least components; like soap bubbles (Sharghi & Ghanbaran, 2008, 111).

1.10.4.2 Plant Structures

Terrestrial plants are divided into two groups: vascular and non-vascular. The vascular plant system consists of wood and phloem tissue, which is responsible for transporting water and soluble wood and phloem for transporting photosynthetic products. In addition to the role of conducting material, these vascular systems are located continuously like vertical columns from the root to the inside of the leaves.

Natural forms have been evolving for billions of years, leaving only the forms in which form and force are always in balance. It seems that the study of cases that involve millions of years of evolution and selection of nature, can provide the basis for solving many engineering problems. Egg shells, grain shells, animal skulls, water bubbles, seashells are common examples of shells found in nature. A good example of the use of shells in nature are oysters, which have simple mathematical functions. Gastropods are a family of oysters that often have a spiral shape. The torsional shape of this type of oyster corresponds to a logarithmic or golden spiral curve. Abalone oyster, in addition to removing the spiral form in its shell, is one of the few oysters whose plan is placed on a horizontal plane. This type of oyster has holes in the side edge of its shell that shrink algorithmically along the length of the spiral. The general form of an abalone oyster is shown in Figure 1-20 (Qaruni, Omranipour and Yazdi, 2012).

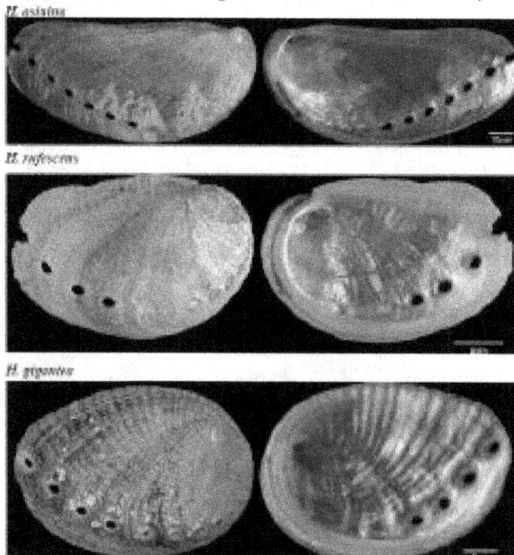

Figure 1.20 The general shape of the abalone oyster and the cavities on the side edge of the skin (Guo, Du-Jiao, 2011: 25)

1.10.4.3 Animal Structures

Animals are the complete stage of nature's existence, which, in addition to the soul, also has tangible movements, which distinguish them from inanimate beings and plants. Animal components such as bones are mainly multifunctional that can convert electrical to mechanical effects and vice versa (piezoelectric property). This feature plays a significant role in the growth and healing of bone fractures. Compressive effects stimulate osteogenic cells to produce bone (in the compression area) and tensile effects cause bone loss (in the elastic region). Therefore, the shape of the bone is in the direction of the force. That is, the bone changes its shape so much (by forming and destroying the bone) that it reduces the flexural anchor and is placed along a force that is compressive. Due to the constant movement, animal forms have stronger relationships than plant counterparts. All the organs of the animal body act in harmony during the movement maneuvers and make a balance in the overall structure. The role of bony organs in the body of animals is mechanically similar to the load-bearing skeleton of a building. Every structure needs a structural skeleton for balance and stability (Sharghi & Ghanbaran, 2008, 112).

1.10.5 Discuss the Effect of some Teachings of Nature on Architectural Design

The teachings of nature have always influenced architectural design. In the following, some categories of the influence of nature on architecture will be discussed:

1.10.5.1 The Geometry of Golden Proportions

In many contemporary architectural designs, geometry is formed only by chance or play with shapes. Reasons for the formation of geometry in nature is an effective aid to the formation of geometry in architecture. Nature is based on special proportions and sizes so that we subconsciously feel that whatever conforms to these dimensions is beautiful and otherwise unpleasant. One of the most important geometric patterns in the structure of all four categories of beings is the combination of two types of free and regular geometry in it. In inanimate, the geometry of clouds or mountain streaks has an unpredictable shape that is governed by perfectly regular and predictable principles and patterns (Kish, Durrani and Mir Sharghi, 2014).

1.10.5.2 Adaptation to Climate

Most desert plants, due to the lack of sufficient water in the upper parts of the soil, have long roots that sink deep into the ground to get the water the plants need. Some desert plants have thick skin, few or no leaves and are equipped with thorns that prevent the evaporation of their internal water. Others have fleshy leaves that can store large amounts of water and consume during the dry seasons. Cactus shrinks during sleep, reducing exposure to the sun. There is a species of this plant that 80% of it is water (Kish, Durrani and Mir Sharghi, 2014).

In cold, hot and dry climates, the plant sections are thick and solid. The outer surface, which contains the solid part and the kernel of the plant, is low. In this case, the plant's kernel is more protected from the cold and scorching heat, and is more balanced than the plant surface with changes in exterior temperature. On the contrary, the plants of temperate regions, in combination with the environmental conditions of different seasons, have a state of freedom. Growing plants in warm and humid areas also varies in shape and size (Sharghi & Ghanbaran, 2008).

Animals also have different behavioral and structural adaptations in nature. For example, two-humped camels with high wool can withstand the cold of the mountains, but one-humped camels due to their special physiological structure are resistant to high heat, but in cold below 15 degrees need shelter. The body of this animal is narrow in the upper part of the waist, so in the hottest hours of the day when the sun shines completely vertically, a small surface of its body is in contact with direct sunlight. Camel hump also has two different functions: As a heat insulator against the scorching sun and another one is the store of energy and water. When fat is burned, hydrogen is released and combined with oxygen in the air, produces water, and about 21 liters of water is obtained from 20 kg of fat (Kish, Durrani and Mir Sharghi, 2014).

1.10.5.3 Nature Structures in the Process of Measurement and the Cycle of Modification

In areas where there are always strong winds, the roots of the trees are stronger so that they can withstand the anchor caused by the lateral force of the wind. Under these conditions, the root usually grows in the opposite direction of the wind to provide the necessary tensile inhibition. In these areas, the middle core of the tree trunk is bent in the opposite direction and the annual rings become more compact than the tensile section in the part where the applied force creates compressive stress (Senoozian, 2010).

Over time, designers try to create more dynamism in their designs. The single organic style in architecture is the result of taking advantage of this natural law. According to Calatrava, buildings can also be changing as part of nature. Calatrava in the canopy is a metaphor for flight and bird wings (Nazar Nia, 2008).

1.10.5.4 Preserving Identity in Nature

In nature, species are self-conscious and reproduce only in the same range. In plants, grafting is possible between different plants, but it is not common. Each plant can only be grafted to plants of the whole family.

In art and architecture, the inherent characteristics of the species must be preserved as well. In today's architecture, many times, different identities are combined and create heterogeneous forms (Kish, Durrani and Mir Sharghi, 2014).

1.10.5.5 Existence of Details at Different Scales

In nature, there is a level at the same level according to the scale. In architecture, buildings that can be understood from different distances, there should be proportional distances at different levels, scales and details. Architecture that lacks detail can quickly become tedious and boring, and the best solution to this problem is to study nature's approach to the problem (Sharghi & Ghanbaran, 2008).

1.10.6 Summary of Subject of Nature

Man's attempt to change or adapt to nature to create a structure has always been questionable. Man's subconscious imitation of nature has resulted in the payment of interest and ransom as well as benefits. The interdependence of these two phenomena is defined by biological processe. Architecture, like any other science, is highly efficient and nurtures architectural architects who come up with powerful solutions to their goals. A new bionic approach to the exterior of buildings has brought nature and the building more in harmony. Nature-inspired ideas for architecture make the form of components and forces more combined and harmonious. These components may not be visible but no longer (building and nature) does not seem irrelevant. The relationship between nature and architecture is similar to its biological climax, and to some extent it eliminates shortcomings. It is possible to neutralize the shortcomings of human life in harmony and coordination with nature.

Chapter 2:

Bionic architecture

2.1 Bionic Approach

After the Industrial Revolution, using scientific discoveries and the laws of nature, man was able to discover their secrets and use them to inspire industrial projects. The term "bionic" was first coined in the mid-twentieth century to use biological studies in the technical, industrial design, and materials sciences. Bionic formation is an attempt to strike a reasonable and realistic balance between man and nature; a balance that, inspired by nature, meets human needs and ensures the health of nature alongside ecological systems. The ancient philosopher Aristotle was one of the first to mention nature as a great and inspiring resource. He stated that functional beauty exists even in very small creatures.

Nature is like an engineering office that has conducted try and error for millions of years and has discovered the best answers that fit its needs. This problem-solving method can be a reliable source for inspiration in solving engineering problems. Considering the global trend of environmental protection as well as the willingness to work on the issue of sustainable development has led to the spread of bionic science. However, in the field of architecture, although research on environmentally friendly and green design has increased, most of this research has been done in terms of materials. The use of bionics in architecture and design seems to be a new and contemporary idea. Related research in bionic studies has been done mainly by Westerners (Ghiabakloo, 2013).

2.1.1 The Concept of Bionics

The word "bionic" is a combination of the words "biology" and "technology". Bionics is an interdisciplinary science between materials sciences, biology, and engineering, in which lessons learned from nature become the basis of engineering. In this science, the study of biological structures, the creation of relationships between properties and structure in order to develop processing methods and microstructural design for new materials. Researchers over the past two decades have made significant efforts to elucidate the structure and mechanisms beyond these mechanical functions in order to reproduce them in synthetic materials. Sarikaya divides this science into two parts:

- Biomimetics: Understanding biological systems and using these concepts in artificial applications using current technology;
- Biodeplication: It is a more advanced stage in which new methods such as genetic engineering are used to produce a class of new materials (Sarikaya, 1994: 360).

In recent years, the biomimetics approach has been used as a mechanism for technological advancement. Researchers define parameters based on similarities between natural systems and engineering ones. The limitations of inspiration, however, depend on structural and mechanical differences. The goal of biomimetics is the production of engineering systems that have the characteristics, similarities, or functions of living systems. Also to create a reasonable and realistic balance between man and nature; a balance that, given its inspiration from nature, meets human needs and ensures the health of nature alongside ecological systems in the following ways:

- Better use of resources with minimal components;
- Utilizing the minimum energy for construction;
- The right combination of strength and beauty;
- Production capacity instead of mere consumption.

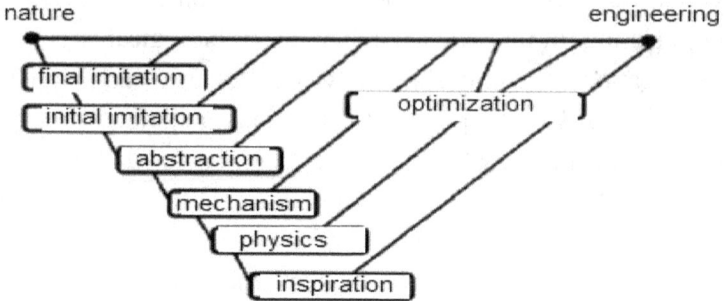

Figure 2.11 Biomimetics diagram, the process of idea to engineering

2.1.2 History of Bionic Science

For centuries, human beings have been in close contact with nature and have been inspired by it to produce their necessities. Renaissance genius Leonardo da Vinci was one of the first to combine "biological" and "technical" knowledge to build a flying machine and to solve problems in his time, he researched and researched the structure of living things. Today, five hundred years after Da Vinci, engineers in various fields are making a similar effort to make the connection between the laws of technical science and the world of living things. A relationship that has gained a special place with the beginning of the 21st century and the increasing growth of computers and has also affected the world of architectural ideas (Golabchi et al. 2014: 43). Large volume of articles, lectures, theoretical topics presented in the past few years is the confirmation of this claim. Along with the culmination of these discussions, you can also see the presentation of the outstanding works of this movement in the halls of the world's prestigious museums. We see one of the first uses of natural creations for architectural innovation in the early second half of the nineteenth century. In 1846, English specialists for the first time succeeded in breeding a huge lotus in Europe with a diameter of two meters. Paxton, the English architect, saw the strength of the leaves of this lotus and studied the circular shelving and radial structure of this flower. The result of this research was the invention of a new structure for the light glass ceiling in architecture, which was presented at the Crystal Palace of the London World's Fair in 1851 and succeeded in attracting the attention of critics (Figure 2.3) (Golabchi et al. 2014: 55).

We also see other cases such as cooperation and interdisciplinary study of the structure of human femurs to build light and low-cost structures in the nineteenth century. Beginning in the twentieth century (the pre-modern era) and then the early modern years, we come across more or less similar efforts, which remain more theoretical. Le Corbusier's interest in oystercatchers and the study of the structure of these creatures can be an example in this regard.

Figure 2.22 Influence of English architect Pakston on lotus flower in designing the roof of London Crystal Palace

2.1.3 Bionic Science and Achievement of Nature for the Contemporary World

Bionic, biology or use of artificial organs in nature, was first discovered by the American scientist Jack. E. Steel was used in 1960. He considers bionics to be the science of systems that are the foundation of all living systems. At first, Bionic studied machines that were designed and built based on living systems, but now it is the art of applying the knowledge of living systems to solve technical problems. Nowadays, wherever we talk about technology, the image of the same important technological achievements that meet the basic needs of human beings for today and future, comes to mind. But if we pay a little attention to the direction of technology, we will more or less find out the origin of some phenomena, for example, which industrial or construction phenomenon each living pattern of nature is inspired by. For years, researchers have been trying to prove the causality and existence of this relationship through which to study and justify the formation of different systems of life. And from the results of this research, by combining the two words "biology" and "technique", they have established the science of "bionics" as a science that solves technical problems via biological means (Figure 4.2) (Golabchi et al. 2014: 37).

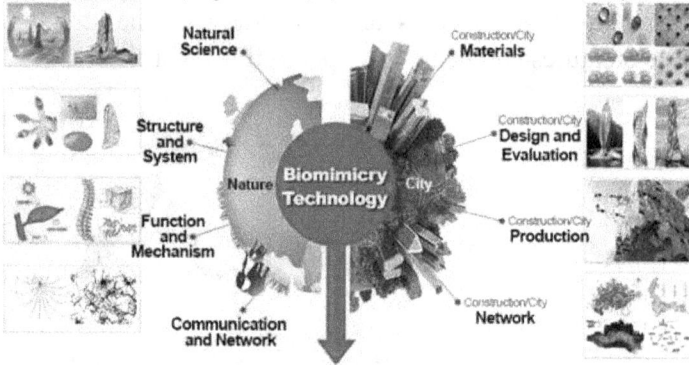

Figure 2.23 The structure of bionic science and its impact on various areas of life

2.1.4 Design Process in Bionic

In general, the design steps based on nature and biodesign patterns are as follows:

1- Selection of living things (desired phenomenon in nature)

- Animals
- Plants
- Diatoms, single cells

2- Identify biological characteristics

- Living environment: environmental conditions, temperature, humidity, pressure and sound;

- Reactions: vital resources, respiratory systems, food;
- Physical characteristics: coexistence conditions, direct and indirect compatibility and incompatibility;
- Systematic relationships: Cumulative statistics and biodistribution, specific geographical conditions.

3- Identify architectural features

- Internal structures;
- Systematic relationships;
- Available main body: micro elements and geometric proportions, macro elements, materials and ratios.

Bionic architecture in the process of creation; adapts to the location of the building, common local styles, climatic conditions, building materials and local perception of beauty (Hagan, S, 2001).

2.1.5 Bionic Architecture

The word bionic is derived from the Greek words bios (life) and ecos (unit), which means living unit. A term that refers to all artificial structures designed from living systems (Senoozian, 2010).

Bionic, meaning biologically using the artificial limbs of nature, was first used by an American scientist in 1959. He considers bionics to be the science of systems that are the foundation of all living systems, the science that solves technical problems through biological means (Mahmoodi Nejad, 2009: 395).

In bionics, the goal is to use the conversion of different energies to each other in a way other than conventional physical and mathematical methods. That is, by modeling the phenomena of energy conversion in living organisms. As an example of the power of converting the sun's light energy into chemical energy in the green leaves of trees (Mahmoodi nejad, 2009: 401). Revitalizing the building is one of the tendencies of bionic architecture that the designers of this field achieve due to the power of the structure to breathe (revitalization) with the help of straight lines or pure curves and slow induction of the integrity of the structure. And the most important thing for bionic architects is that the building can inspire its liveliness (Mahmoodi Nejad, 2009: 399).

Buildings in the past were built in bionic architecture either using fragile and unstable materials or in the heart of the earth and rocks. One of these natural places was caves. Of course, the architecture of the cave, which is mainly in the heart of the architecture of the tombs, has existed since ancient times.

These buildings are probably housed something like large termite nests. In addition, mud or earthy architecture can be considered as one of the branches of natural architecture. Ancient and historic cities such as Sanaa in Yemen or the mud buildings (Dogon) in Mali are examples of this style. Nature-inspired cottages in the woods of the Native Amazons, or in the huts of the Eskimos or Alaska, are inspired by nature (Kish, Durrani and Mir Sharghi, 2014).

Greg Lane, one of the leaders in bionic architecture, wanted to create buildings that had a lot of flexibility to adapt to nature and the natural environment. One of the most famous works of this architect is his embryonic house, which is an attempt to create an architectural behavior: single production versus mass production, related to modernity (Mahmoodi Nejad, 2009: 399). Charlie Luxton, one of the pioneers in the field of bionic architecture, considers the focus of bionic architects to be the use of things in nature that strengthen the building and create variety and tranquility in the space. Animal balance is an important principle that architects have been inspired by in their designs, including Calatrava, a feature that is abundant in his work (Mahmoodi, 2009, 262).

2.1.6 Stages of Designing Bionic Architecture

The use of optimized natural forms and modeling them in the construction of architectural and building forms can, in addition to reducing time and cost, provide the necessary flexibility to design the shell and create new forms in the field of architectural design. In the late nineteenth century, Darcy Thompson founded the science of morphology. In her two-volume book (On Growth and Form), she showed that natural shapes and structures were formed and created on the basis of the principle of survival and the desire for organisms to survive, in spite of diversity, complexity, elegance, richness and beauty. In his book Anatomy of Nature, Andreas Fanynger also considers the evolution of structure and form in nature as a conscious response to survival. In fact, the natural form and structure is the result of a continuous flow of adaptation to environmental forces. Bionic design is a movement that began in the 1960s. However, due to technical limitations such as the lack of advanced microscopes, the lack of simulation software, advanced optimization, etc., it did not have a significant impact in those years.

After studies, the proposed steps for designing bionic architecture are as follows: (Figure 2.5)

- o Step 1: Define and identify the problem form;
- o Step 2: Analysis and interpretation of the problem form;
- o Step 3: Search to find and discover natural, living, and biological solutions;
- o Step 4: Introduction to natural and biological solutions;
- o Step 5: Extraction of natural, living, biological principles and imitation;
- o Step 6: Evaluate, measure and apply principles and foundations.

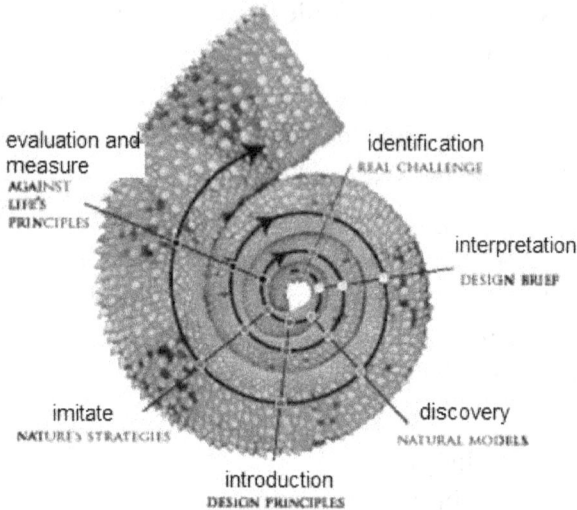

evaluation and measure
AGAINST LIFE'S PRINCIPLES

identification
REAL CHALLENGE

interpretation
DESIGN BRIEF

imitate
NATURE'S STRATEGIES

discovery
NATURAL MODELS

introduction
DESIGN PRINCIPLES

Figure 2.24 Suggested steps for designing bionic architecture
(http://www.biomimicryinstitute.org)

In general, it can be said that bionic design is a convergent design. This means that going through any of these steps does not mean the end of the stage, and in a spiral motion and based on the need and design process, there is a return to the previous stages.

- Step 1: Define and identify the problem form

This stage is the most important part of the design stages of bionic architecture and consists of three parts: question assumption, performance analysis, and performance optimization. The designer defines the problem with an in-depth look at the possible assumptions and interpretations. In the past, the most important problem was the lack of tools and software for analysis, but now, with the development of software and tools, including scanning microscopes, much progress has been made.

- Step 2: Analyzing and interpreting the problem statement includes the following steps:

- Ask biologists about nature's view of the problem;
- Translate design performance into nature performance;
- How nature overcomes the problem;
- Redefining hypotheses and initial questions by considering findings and adding keywords.
- Step 3: Search to find and discover natural, living, biological solutions
- Search for an organism in nature that has answered and solved the problem well
- Step 4: Introduction to natural, living, biological solutions
- Find repetitive patterns and processes in nature that are successful by definition;
- Choose the most appropriate strategy to challenge the design;
- Summarize the list of principles that led nature to success;
- Step 5: Extraction of natural, living, biological principles and imitation
- Expand ideas and solutions, based on natural models;
- Imitation of form: finding the principles of morphology, recognizing the effect of scale, considering the factors affecting the form of the organism;
- Imitation of performance: considering the details of the biological process, considering the factors affecting the effectiveness of the process for the organism;
- Ecosystem mimicry: Considering the factors affecting the effectiveness of the process for living things;
- Evaluate, measure and apply principles and foundations (Qaruni, Omranipour and Yazdi, 2012).

2.1.7 Features of Bionic Architecture

Enlivening the building is one of the bionic architectural tendencies that the designers of this field achieve due to the strength of the structure to breathe (revitalization), with the help of straight lines or pure curves and slow induction of the integrity of the structure. The most important principle in bionic architecture is that the building can evoke its own vitality. In general, the following important factors and elements that exist in nature and have been used by humans to build their buildings, can be mentioned as follows:

- Shell or cover;
- Structure;
- Arrangement;
- Energy.

Bionic and naturalistic architects take a new look at structures. Just as genetic language uses codes with specific shapes and forms to understand the relationship between phenomena, computers can be used here to simulate the shape of living things with structures and architecture. Architecture can be called the science of artificial life. The most important achievement of organic and bionic mentality (Senoozian, 2010: 25).

2.1.8 Biomimetic Architecture

Biomimetics is the science of imitating living organisms to design intelligent materials and builders. After studying the skeletal tissues of plants and animals, it becomes clear that one of the characteristics of biological systems is that they are made up of a limited number of molecules, but these materials are very diverse in terms of microscopic structure. In order to imitate nature, man began to build composite systems. The important point is that only in the last thirty years has man started to make composite materials (composite) imitating nature. And this is while man-made materials before that were homogeneous materials (like steel) (Mahmoodi Nejad, 2009, 414).

Biological systems are a rich resource for scientists looking to build new materials and processes (Mahmoodi Nejad 2009, 417).

Table 2.2 An example of a biomimetic application framework (Ghiabakloo, 2013)

Example of a building that mimics termites	The method of imitation	Imitation level
A building that looks like a termite	Shape	Structure and organs
A building made of materials similar to a termite organ, such as its skin or skeleton	Material	
A building that has different growth cycles like termites	How to built	
A building that, like termites, constantly has enough water available by combining air oxygen with hydrogen (recycling waste such as waste into biogas and wastewater on site)	Process	
A building made of recycled materials, such as termite function (which converts cellulose waste into soil)	Performance	
The building has been built by a termite and its shape is similar to a termite nest	Shape	Individual behavior
A building whose materials are similar to those of a termite nest	Material	
A building rised by the termite construction method (digging and constructing floors)	How to built	
A building that, like a termite nest, has the most appropriate direction, shape and materials	Process	
A building whose internal conditions are always at an optimal temperature in terms of thermal conditions	Performance	
A building that resembles the ecosystem in which termites live	Shape	Ecosystem and
A building that is built from the natural	Material	

resources of the ecosystem in which the termites live.		
A building that, like the termite ecosystem, benefits from the principles of sequence and complexity over time.	How to built	
A building that, like the termite ecosystem, receives energy from the sun and stores water	Process	
A building that, like the termite ecosystem, exploits the connection between the water cycle, carbon and nitrogen	Performance	

Projects such as the Guggenheim Museum (1991) by Frank O. Gehry, which after making the original mud model, were designed entirely in the computer 3D virtual world or projects like Max Reinhard House (1992) by Peter Eisenman who used sophisticated software systems to deliver primitive forms based on nonlinear mathematical algorithms but in the meantime, Lane uses the computer in a different way. He was one of the first architects to give a creative role to the computer. It is the computer that "under the artist's supervision" creates new works that are created based on approximate equations. His design begins with the breakdown of a work into subsets.

One of the most famous works of this architect is his "Embryonic House" which he designed in 2000. This plan is an attempt to deal with issues such as "diversity", "individual production" alongside "production" and "flexibility" in construction. This house is a combination of different members, all of rules are geometrically defined and their range of growth is specified as well. The architect says: it shows me that appropriateness, beauty, and performance are invaluable in their classic sense but I must also note that I create these qualities with a new tool and a new feeling. These rules ultimately do not allow both to be the same. The embryonic house in its evolutionary path is not only affected by the initial data but also more importantly in the process of creation; it adapts to the location of the building, common local styles, climatic conditions, building materials and local perception of beauty (Hagan, 2001).

Here we consider the effect of natural knowledge on the theorist. If an animal (for example a bear) manages to adapt not only its diet but also its physical structure and even its color and skin to different conditions in different places and climatic conditions from Asia and the Americas to the North Pole, why can't an architectural work achieve such an conformation? The hallmark of his discourse is the lack of definition of a "privileged species", an "optimal breed" or a defined framework in general. He tends to show architects the process and "path of optimization" and the "process of species" and to offer a new and unknown understanding of beauty. He does not define major constraints for the creation of his work, but it is the elements of his work, based on data and conditions set in the virtual world of computers, grow in his authorized realm and create optimal quality for specific conditions but beyond all defined geometric boundaries and common architectural frameworks.

2.2 Starfish as an Example of a Bionic Structure

The most common trait of animals, which first appears during the developmental stages, is their structural level. All animals start life from a single cell, and some do not go above the tissue level, but others go through it and will have more complex body. Thus, animals (metazoa) are considered to have two branches of classification. In the Parazoa branch, the highest structural level is the texture. This set only includes sponge group. All other animals are belonged to the Yomtazoa branch which are identified by their limbs and apparatus.

The second general trait that appears after the building level during the growth of animals is the type of symmetry. In the beginning, the embryo of all animals has a radial symmetry, ie in the form of a solid or hollow sphere and consists of a number of cells. Some groups of animals, such as the mermaid, maintain this radial symmetry until adulthood but in the rest, after a while, the fetus turned into the secondary radial symmetry (such as a starfish) or bilateral symmetry. The resulting larvae and adult animals usually maintain the same type of symmetry. Accordingly, the Yomatazoa can be divided into two categories: Radial symmetry (Radiata) and Bilateral symmetry (Bilateria).

2.2.1 Type of Symmetry in a Starfish

Most are characterized by having a device and bilateral symmetry after the embryonic stages. Most animals with bilateral symmetry maintain this type of symmetry, but in a few groups, such as starfish; as they deform and mature, have the secondary radial symmetry. Five or more arms protruding from the center of its body, create a radial symmetry in the animal's body. In fact, the bodies of starfish ancestors are said to have had a two-way symmetry, with modern starfish still retaining remnants of the same body structure. Such adult animals, like animals with radial symmetry, become sedentary, static and headless.

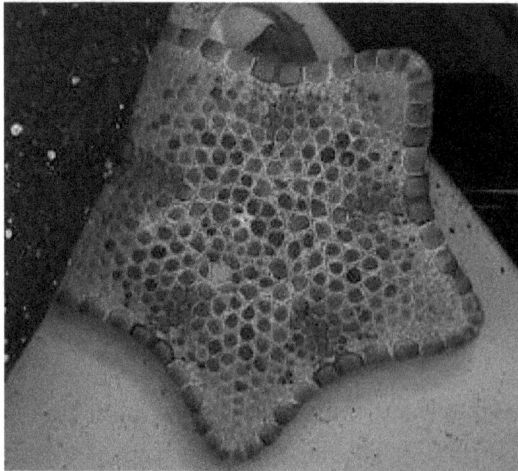

Figure 2.25 Symmetry in the starfish

Figure 2.26 Symmetry in the starfish

2.2.1.1 Starfish Ossification

Bones are the skeletal frame components of animals that carry their body weight. Therefore, they can be compared to the structures consisting of beams and columns used in the large modern buildings. Components of this skeletal frame that are not structurally efficient and only increase the weight of the skeleton will be phased out. The Spanish architect and engineer Santiago Calatrava has inspired nature in many of his designs and has designed structures in the shape of animal skeletons. Examples include the entrance building to Lyon Airport in France and the Lusitania Bridge in Merida, Spain (Polano, 1996).

Figure 2.27 An example of an novel form in architecture and structure using the shape of an animal skeleton, the terminal building of Lyon Airport, France

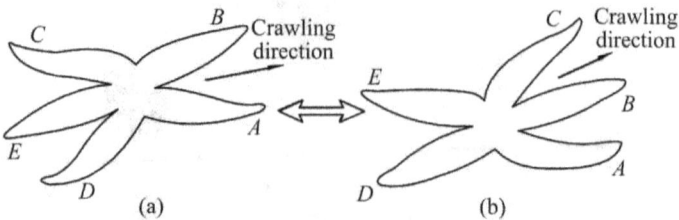

Figure 2.28 The skeleton of a bird

2.2.2 Bionic Structural Systems

In this section, some systems of bionic structures with natural pattern are examined.

2.2.2.1 Construction System

In nature, a large number of starfish movements are recorded as follows (figure 2.17) (Sadr, 2016).

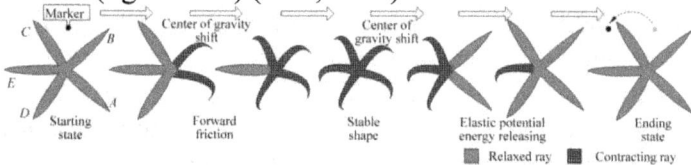

Figure 2.29 Column construction system

The strength and stability of these natural structures can be explained by a set of characteristics: The reciprocal arrangement of hard and soft tissue in the stalk causes an astonishing reaction to pressure and tension. Cereal stalk, such as the ankle and its protrusions, show elasticity. A strong wind can only bend weak stalks. A tree resists the wind by its roots and may break. Skyscrapers were built based on these studies (Figure 2.18) (Sadr, 2016).

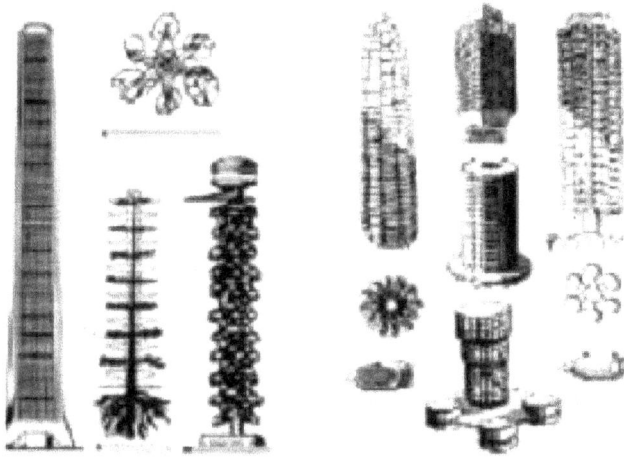

Figure 2.30 Strength and stability of buildings naturally

2.2.2.2 Layered Structure

Dome-shaped buildings are easily found by searching the environment: Eggs, seeds, leaves, marine animals and lice, etc.). These structures bend in space with thin walls. Due to their smooth shape and restless properties, they can spread the force evenly.

An example of a unique and ideal structure with respect to structural stability is the starfish. The only feature of this structure is not its geometric shape. These types of structures are perhaps the patterns of the widest structures with large spaces with long distances between the main supports (pavilions, cinemas, theaters, sports fields, etc.). These structures require small amounts of materials. Almost all of them are light and the thickness of the side walls is only a few millimeters (Figure 2.19) (Sadr, 2016).

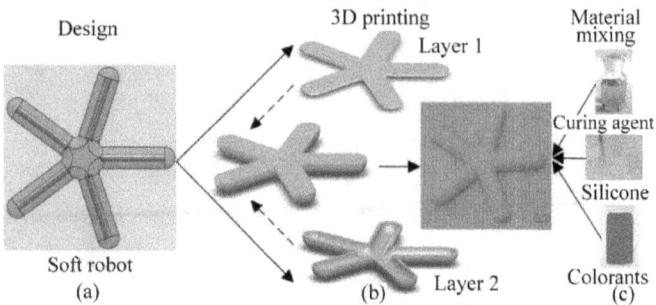

Figure 2.32 Layered patterns inspired by natural elements

Figure 2.33 Structures with elastic cable

2.2.2.3 Buildings Composed of Geometric Shapes

Nature is the source of hexagonal and triangular shapes that can be seen in spherical cells or bubbles. However, they are a collection of complex natural compounds and structures or other forms. These shapes can take on a new shape under pressure with axes up to 120 degrees (Sadr, 2016). These models are elastic surfaces and they have some tensile capabilities. Polygonal shapes can be seen on the skin of giraffes or tortoiseshells, and other types can be seen on the inner parts of starfish.

Unicellular animals or microscopic plankton live in saltwater and some in the ocean. The appearance of a protozoan is generally spherical, which is a combination of bone silicon, strontium, or bone elements that flow inside the cell. This bone network is like detached bubbles. Energy levels in a hexagonal environment, sometimes porous, are reduced so that the cytoplasm can store and strengthen nutrients (Sadr, 2016). Fouler believed that the best network structure with a spherical, hexagonal or triangular shape is called a dome (Figure 2.21). A dome building is formed of quadrilateral geometric surfaces; like a sphere or a dome that never changes shape. This structure is stable, rigid, symmetrical, regular, and proportionate and with a simple composition that includes notable elements. In other words, this structure is a compound that is easily made in a short time and cheaply.

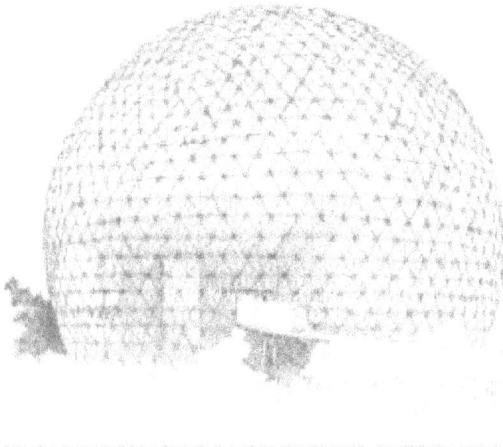

Figure 2.34 Buildings composed of geometric shapes

2.2.3 Nature and Efficient Operation of Buildings (Structures)

Shapes in nature are formed in such a way that they have the best performance and transfer of large amounts of energy using minimal materials. In his book (On Growth and Shapes), Thompson says: The living space of living things is formed as a result of coordination and adaptation to physical forces.

In his book (Anatomy of Nature), Finings says that evaluating the shape of a building is an intelligent reaction in life (Sadr, 2016). In fact, form and structure are the result of relationships with environmental powers. Natural structures usually have layers of tissue in which these deformations are caused by pressure and cause elastic or compressive reactions. This issue is seen in the stalks of wheat or strong trees and is used in the construction of airplanes and skyscrapers, which is called the monochromic system.

On the other hand, all natural structures must be stable when exposed to the physical force of tension. As an example, we can consider the spider web, which is a network of threads on which the spider and its prey can be considered as the axis of pressure. The next example is the elastic structure in Munich in which elastic networks of steel strands and large steel beams withstand pressure (Figure 2.35) (Sadr, 2016).

Figure 2.35 elastic structure

In the world of construction, it benefited from the most operations using the least materials. Some of the most important examples of this successful mechanism are the Munich Stadium and the Diplomat Club in Riyadh (Figure 2.36 and 2.37) (Sadr, 2016).

Figure 2.36 Munich Stadium

Figure 2.37 Diplomat Club in Riyadh

2.2.3.1 Nature and Structural Beauty

Natural shapes are basically useful and have taken advantage of patterns. In nature, there is attention to desirability and beauty. However, in the engineering world, the use of patterns in a design based on beauty is not always successful. Attaching a template to natural shapes and templates can remove this flaw. A visual understanding of natural shapes is crucial in the development of man-made basic structures.

The reason why an ordinary person may not like a perfectly correct design is because they have never seen anything like it in nature. Although the arch is aesthetically valuable, its frame is neither beautiful nor ugly. This design is outside the world of art. In the natural environment, concave objects and elements are almost common. Scalloped shapes are not only a symbol for protection but they are also considered as a beauty element (Sadr, 2016).

Dumb buildings, despite the light, look heavy and are compared to ancient stone dome roofs that do not allow the structure and movement (circulation) to be understood and cause distress to people. This kind of confusion or distress never happens when it comes to camping; because some of their symbols exist on a small scale in nature. An example of the connection between nature, science, and perofmrance is the Ludwig building in Berlin, Germany, built by Nicolas GrimShaw, a great symbol of this type of building. The repetition of the oval arches was inspired by the badger's nesting. In such a way that rooms on different floors are located around a vestibule or middle room, with free floor (Figure 2.25) (Sadr, 2016).

A bridge with architectural fractures directs the force out of the bridge while a suspension bridge pulls the force inward. According to this item, a bridge can be designed based on reducing these forces, such as the Albert Bridge building in the UK (1859). The design of a building with lighting equals the design of a suspension bridge. This compound was used millions of years ago in the skeletons of living things (Sadr, 2016).

(Figure 2.38) Albert Bridge Building

The best example of a suspension bridge could be the skeleton of a dinosaur called Brontosaurus. The legs of this animal are long and uniform, like a pillar. Their spine acts as an arched roof that transmits force to the legs. So we can store precious materials and use fewer columns (Figure 2.39) (Sadr, 2016).

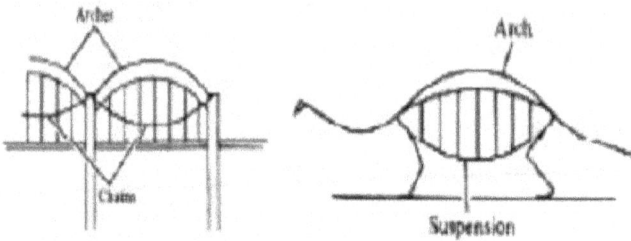

Figure 2.39 the idea of designing a bridge from a dinosaur skeleton

Inspiring of the nature, it is not only used in towers but also in modern buildings like the Swiss Re in London, which is designed like a sea sponge (Figure 2.40). This little creature clings to the seabed and has a perfect silicone skeleton with a perfect geometric shape. This structure helps the wind to flow just like the structure of a sea sponge. Compared to a rectangular shape, it reduces the wind cone. The beauty of this structure is due to modeling based on natural shape (Sadr, 2016).

Figure 2.40 like Osvis Re in London

The design of the London Water Olympics building, for example, was inspired by the water waves of the River Thames. The water center, which was commissioned in the

Stratford area of east London at a cost of about ٣٠٠ million (equivalent to 480 billion tomans), includes two 50-meter pools in addition to a diving pool. After the insulation stage, these pools were carpeted with more than 180,000 turquoise tiles. In the construction of this complex building with an arched roof and two movable wings, about 3360 tons of steel bars have been used. Moving wings open and close according to weather conditions. In addition to the Olympic swimming and diving competitions, the center will also host the final waterpolo games, with 17,500 seats for spectators. After the games, the number of seats will be reduced to 2,500, space will be dedicated for public gatherings, and swimming pools will be used for national and regional competitions.

Figure 2.41 London Water Olympic Building

Figure 2.42 Various views of the London Water Olympic building

The winning team of the London Water Olympics project, led by Zaha Hadid, was selected in 2005 from among 200 volunteer companies across the world that registered to design in London. The wavy roof of this design is a meandering reflection of a river that passes through the middle of the London Olympic Park and is located at the entrance and outside the park, and is a sign of unity and similarity of the people. London Water Stadium opened in 2011. The unique and status-like feature is that it makes it unique and attracts tourists and visitors to East London.

Figure 2.43 Stages of construction of the London Water Olympic building

2.2.4 Summary of the Topic of the Bionic Approach

Man, who has always relied on nature in the construction of weapons and shelter and all the elements of his civilization, has tried in a long process to discover suitable patterns of shelter and housing from. As a result of these efforts, today in a more modern and scientific way in the form of bionic architecture, it is trying to develop this science and attitude, which, of course, has achieved some accomplishments. Many works of world famous architects have been created in this field and it is evolving every day as an idea.

With a respectful view of nature and its manifestations, bionic architecture tries to use natural rules and forms that have been formed over thousands of years and are produced in a sustainable way to create shelter. This view can be divided into more specialized sections in practical work. Supposing that in modeling nature, one can make interpretations of the form, structure, compositions, materials, and the location of natural phenomena. In a building in bionic style, all of these areas or just one of them may be applied. Bionics like sustainability, is not limited to architecture. This science was first formed in other fields and then spread into the architecture. Contrary to popular belief, bionics is not just the application of biological patterns in new technologies, but researchers in the field are trying to complement and apply the desired natural functions. Conscious modeling of samples and mechanisms of natural organisms is a part of bionics in which nature is used as a database of proven solutions. In this field, some specific natural patterns are sometimes used as data sources, but this is part of the whole process that this science is currently following.

2.3 Principles of Architecture of Commercial and Administrative Spaces

2.3.1 Administrative Building

Separate offices for one to three people, with workshops for trainees and group offices for up to 20 people, some of them combine separate workshops with group sections. In an open-plan office, except for a separate secretarial department, the rest of the space is reserved for multi-purpose individual and group work: document storage parts for storing files, plans, microfilm and electronic devices, archiving and recording equipment, recording documents, reconstruction and shredding. Main administrative services, with equipment for writing, duplication, printing, photocopying and personal computers. Post office section, letters and postal items, control of entry and exit of goods, group show section, including meeting rooms with movable walls and exhibition sections, conference and meeting halls for staff, place to eat and drink, sports facilities, dining hall with kitchen. Additional and attached locations, possibly for training in the use of audio-visual equipment, may require a car entry area, parking space (underground) and delivery areas. Group spaces including corridors - stairs - elevators - exit and emergency entrances internally and externally.

Main services include technical service issues, air conditioning, ventilator, heating system, electricity, ideal system, information processing, computer center, telecommunications and cleaning and care; increase the level of necessary infrastructure in offices from approximately 2 to 3 square meters to about 15 to 18 square meters. Impacts of information technology, computerization of official system, advances in information and communication technology; have helped to change the working conditions in the offices. The impact of computerization of the official system on workshops and plans has eliminated needs that existing administrative buildings can no longer meet. Proper design minimizes barriers to the workflow.

2.3.2 Conditions for Administrative Space

The construction of a new administrative building depends on its local location. The building should be built as much as possible in a place that benefits from daylight and away from strong sunlight and heat. In the United States, 90% of administrative buildings are built east-west because sunlight in the afternoon is unpleasant. It is easy to use the canopy to block sunlight from the south. However, if the initial direction is north-south, sunlight will reach all rooms.

2.3.3 The Systems

Building a row of rooms is usually not cost-effective and is only acceptable for the back of the office where sunlight is a problem. The design of regular three-row rooms is for administrative and high-rise buildings.

In buildings that are built without corridors, all the rooms (with natural and artificial light) are gathered around a communication core including elevators, stairs, ventilation ducts, etc. But in other buildings, service areas are marginalized.

You can use sunlight up to 7 meters away from the window. With the use of new systems of daylight technology that direct and change the direction of light (prisms and reflectors), maximum daylight can be used and exploited.

2.3.4 Recognition the Types of Offices

Large administrative buildings are usually multi-storey buildings with internal movable walls. Installation centers such as plumbing, stairs, elevators, etc. are usually within the maximum stages set by the building regulations. For maximum time and continuity of work in administrative environments, installation cores can be placed in front of the building on one side of the building, in the inner corners at the end of a passage, at the bottom of the corridors near the light source. A row of simple central columns creates a corridor on one side or the other. Making a double row of columns creates offices of equal height. In such cases, corridors should be lit directly by high windows or through glass doors inside the wall. Corridors can be illuminated with skylights in side, short, angled, T and U-shaped buildings which is cost-effectively with daylight.

2.3.5 Administrative Space Furniture

The fit of administrative supplies with offices is influenced by factors such as adaptability, adjustment, durability, compatibility, storage space, efficiency, beauty and way of wiring. The space required for employees to sit or stand is the basis for calculating the minimum distance between desks and desks (minimum optimal distance of 10 meters). The seats must be adjustable with wheelchair-equipped, furnished, and equipped with a backrest. Archives, chartulary, and information cards related to universities, etc. can be placed in sideless cabinets, which are usually made of steel and in standard dimensions.

2.3.6 Administrative Building Design Standards

The function of the administrative space is like a large machine in which all its parts must be connected and coordinated with each other and function properly. Every administrative function should be easily and clearly related to other departments, while minimizing friction with them.

The six basic administrative functions are:

1. Management
2. Finance affairs
3. Sales
4. Public services
5. Technical services
6. Produce

1. Management group: which is always concentrated in a range with its own hierarchy. This section is far from public transportation and direct access and can be located in the periphery of offices or in the center. More formal departments can be assigned to management, and naturally the largest and best offices in the executive departments are the management team, due to the greater individuality and clientele.

2. Financial group: although the responsibilities of the financial sector in public administration are extensive and comprise a significant percentage of the clerical workforce, it should be in direct contact with the commodity trading sector. The business sections are client-related and should therefore be close to the reception. Personnel departments should also be located near the reception so that they can be accessed without much movement in the administrative space. Intelligence activities are always at the bottom of the line and should be in a central location away from the hustle and bustle.

3. Sales group: in some departments, a set of sales functions is considered as the main activity and there are important connections between this section and other ones. The sales team has a lot of clients and needs a lot of space (dorost) for catalogs and archives.

4. Public services: this section serves other sections and includes: central archive: typewriting, library, post, telex and fax affairs, printing and duplication, public relations, etc. Reference functions such as: central archive, library and central typing section are generally central to other departments. The letter writing section is also located at the end of the administrative work flow. Due to the noise, the photocopier can be placed near the noisier parts: for example, near the reception and waiting areas. The call center is located in a part of the reception area. In institutions that have a more complex organization, this section can be a separate center and independent of other activities.

5. Technical services department: technical services such as engineering, drawing, design and maintenance are usually located close to the activities they coordinate with, such as production, sales and procurement.

6. Production group: this department is always located in a secondary office that is located outside the institution and is as important as the public sector and should have the same prestige and facilities.

2.4 Study of Organizational Chart

The order of operations of the department will be a form of organization according to which the work flow and physical needs of each department are formed, which is reflected in the organizational charts. The diagram is also the key to finding the connection between the sections.

It is better to place small activities around important administrative activities than to integrate with them. Each section has good reasons to be in one position instead of the other. Here are ten guides to deciding where each section might be located. When each section is in a large range in terms of overall position, it can change in detail in the future without any particular change in the base pattern of the work. And finally, this guide suggests the best and most favorable agreement.

1. Suitable for the general public: Sections that have a large number of clients can be arranged in such a way that the client goes through a short, direct and effortless process from the main entrance to the desired section. Sales, purchasing, hiring, or the private sectors always have the most customers. Proper access not only makes the client comfortable, but also minimizes the inconvenience to employees.

2. Workflow: The sectors that are closest to each other can be closer to. In this case, the work is done in the minimum time. If these departments are too far apart, a lot of energy will be wasted, and domestic telephones will be too busy.

3. Special equipment: Working in some parts requires special equipment that has extensive wiring. Certainly, the sections with this feature, due to possible future expansion, can not be placed next to each other because moving such sectors is highly cost. Some workstations have high-noise equipment, such as typewriting, duplication, audio-visual equipment, and so on. To reduce the inconvenience of these departments to other employees, they should be separated from other departments.

4. Central functions: Departments and facilities that serve the entire office should be centrally located so that they can be easily accessed by users. For example, writing and typography departments, central archives, accounting and secretariat, especially rest rooms, service and buffet rooms.

5. Confidential areas: Certain functions may need to be separated from other parts of the administration and public sections. Central archives, control departments, and law firms are examples of these practices.

6. Conference rooms: Conference rooms should be located in the detailed sections between management and workspace. If the office is ventilated, these rooms can be located in more indoor spaces to allow other spaces to be located on skylights.

7. Service elevators: Receipt and delivery departments, where a large amount of goods are located near the delivery area, should have service elevators due to less waste of time.

8. Delivery: Cargo and postal delivery activities should be adjacent to the entrance and exit.

9. Service facilities: Dining, medical equipment, and rest areas are generally on the lower floors.

10. Ordinary elevators: When an office has more than one floor, it is necessary to install an elevator. It is better for the public sections to be located on the lower floors.

The basis of the infrastructure network (module) in the design of administrative space is the personal position of the employee, along with the desk and the necessary equipment for them. Open administrative space for each employee should have the ability to enable them to shape their area to the desired shape. In offices and departments that have a system with a specific procedure, space standards must be economical. Where the work is private and has a large clientele, as well as in cases where a special spirit is desired, the space can be large. In public offices, 100 square feet (9.3 square meters) is provided for each employee. 65 square feet (6.04 square meters) is an economic standard for every employee. 80 square feet (7.4 square meters) for each employee can be considered the desired average.

2.4.1 Design of Spaces

Figure 3.1

2.4.2 Stores

Stores are usually located in crowded malls and places where private and public vehicles travel. Car parking standards in the UK include the rule of 3/5-5/25 car space per 10's of retail space (3-4 shifts per day). In the USA, a maximum of 150 cars per acre of land is considered.

2.4.3 Access Route (Passages)

Traffic on sidewalks, vehicles and material distribution vehicles must be done separately. Shopping malls are best limited to sidewalks, walkways (covered for sun and rain), parking lots, and shops. Bus or subway stations may be adjacent to the business center and have direct access to it. The maximum distance between the stopping place of buyers' cars or bus stations and the underground railway is 310m and the road system must have an internal distribution.

2.4.3.1 Space Allocation

Department stores may have exhibitions, restaurants, cafes, kindergartens, banks, post offices, travel agencies, cinemas and gardens. Smaller shops in the mall are often categorized. The design of the shop or the allocation of space to the units begins and must comply with fire and other building regulations. Then, the spaces allocated to the units are again divided into the internal parts of sales areas, internal service areas, common services, etc.

2.4.3.2 Sales Areas

Sales areas should be located immediately above the unit as close to the entrance floor as possible. Using the basement for sale is better than the upper floors. Therefore, warehouses and staff should be located on the upper floors and administrative offices on the uppest floors.

Height of floors

Floor height is 4000-5000 mm for large units and 3000 mm for small units and depends on the type of services (UK method). The high height between the floors is deterrent for customers and tedious for employees. The shops do not rely on natural light, but provide artificial light with mechanical ventilation.

Structural Network

The dimensions and center of the store columns determine the general design of its accessories and furniture. The network of proposed structures for large units has a width of 7300 and 9000 mm and a depth of 9150 mm. The south façade with a frontage of small shops is between 5300 and their depth is 18 to 36 meters (distance from the south façade to the wall behind the store).

Passages

The minimum recommended width for the main passage is 1980 mm and for the sub-passages is 990 mm. The height of the counters is generally 930 mm. The modulus or coefficient of the system varies depending on the type of store shelving.

Moving between Store Floors

The number and width of stairs and exits are determined by building regulations. In the UK, the number of stairs depends on the movement distances of the width of the stairs, and the exits depend on the population density. For example, in the UK method, the load is calculated this way: in the case of ordinary goods, a level of 1.9 m^2 is considered for each person; in special shops, the gross area for each person is about 7 m^2.

There are various rules for building multi- and one-storey small stores. Under UK regulations, with the exception of one-story units, shop buildings must be subdivided into spaces smaller than 7080 (fire regulations). This prevents the construction of very large stairs. And makes it difficult to use escalators and restrict sewer pipes between more than 3 floors. In the USA, determine population density and use national and local codes: Buildings are classified according to use and fire regulations: roofless floor is suitable for sprinkler systems, fire extinguishers and special outlets, etc.

Most customers use escalators but elevators are also at their service. The number of customers who want to go up the ground to the top floor is obtained from this equation: number of floors × store area × population density rate (80% use escalators and 20% use elevators). This figure must be divided by the capacity of the transmission system to obtain the required number of elevators and escalators.

Elevators

The elevators must be in a group and be visible from the entrance. In large stores and in the center of the building, the distance of the elevator from any of the sellers should not be more than 50 meters. Elevators can be grouped back to back or used centrally with escalators.

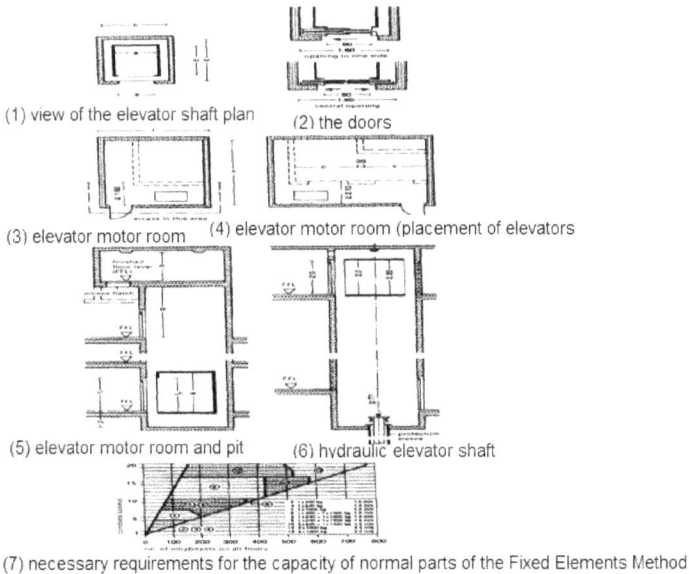

(1) view of the elevator shaft plan   (2) the doors

(3) elevator motor room   (4) elevator motor room (placement of elevators

(5) elevator motor room and pit   (6) hydraulic elevator shaft

(7) necessary requirements for the capacity of normal parts of the Fixed Elements Method

Figure 3.2 Location plan

Escalators

An escalator is required when the number of people being transferred reaches about 2,000 per hour. The escalator must move in both directions and consecutively pass through all the special sales floors of the store building.

The best place is the center of the store floor so that it can be seen from all entrances and its slope is 30^5. In the UK, escalators may be enclosed to comply with fire regulations. But in the USA, it is usually free of any rules.

The fatigue room is often upstairs and includes a kitchen and a storage room lift.

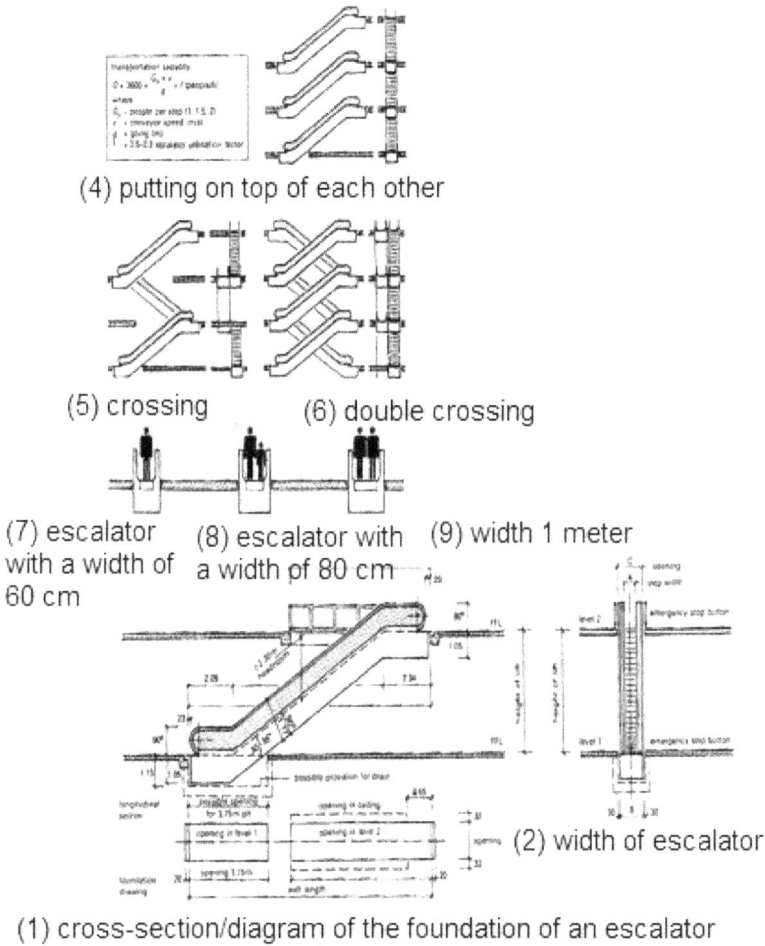

(4) putting on top of each other

(5) crossing   (6) double crossing

(7) escalator   (8) escalator with   (9) width 1 meter
with a width of   a width of 80 cm
60 cm

(2) width of escalator

(1) cross-section/diagram of the foundation of an escalator

Figure 3.3

2.4.4 Distribution of Goods

The delivery route is separate from the customers' movement route and delivery is usually done in the yard containing the goods or by sloping routes. Delivery of goods may be through a warehouse that (perhaps by automatic conveyors) is connected to a public warehouse. If it is difficult to deliver goods on a busy street, it is recommended to use parking spaces. The circulation of the delivered goods starts from the receiving areas (such as warehouses, etc.) and is texted at the place of sale. Disposable materials and rubbish should be taken from the back of the store to the landfill.

Extra goods

Extra goods are stored on one floor, preferably upstairs, or either in a backyard warehouse or on short, half-low floors. Transportation of goods is done by means such as cart, lifting device, sloping duct, roller conveyor, conveyor belt, sloping conveyor, helical duct, hook lift.

WC for Employees

At least one toilet for every 25 women and one toilet for every 25 men, and this rule applies to up to 100 employees. From 100 people up, one toilet should be added for every 40 employees. But a ratio of 15 to 1 increase with increasing the toilet is recommended. Employees are required to provide drinking water, rest areas, a wardrobe area, a machine and drying facilities for outdoor clothing, temperature control, ventilation and lighting, and a chair (according to UK regulations).

Building Regulations

In the case of buildings; equipment and type of wall surfaces of shops and stores, refer to building regulations. In the UK, roofless areas on the wall (such as windows, etc.) must comply with appropriate fire regulations. The floor of the shop and store should be divided according to fire regulations and all vertical roads between the floors should be blocked. The height between store floors is determined by the general building regulations and its boundaries are determined by these regulations. The minimum height of special sales areas should be 3000 mm.

Fire

Special fire-fighting equipment includes: smoke detectors, automatic alarm systems, sprinklers. If sprinklers are used, the desired size of the space is selected twice.

Temperature and Ventilation

The minimum temperature will be after the first hours of operation (UK regulations). Larger units should be ventilated by exhaust and air intake impellers or by air conditioning system. In designing the heating system, the heat from the lighting system of the store and people and goods should be considered.

2.4.4.1 General Plan of the Shop

Like a showcase, the shop must be designed to attract the customer at a glance. The space required for customers and employees depends on the size of the goods and the number of customers. The goal is to use a convenient and fast method. Structures for department stores design a system that meets their specific needs.

2.4.4.2 Location of Shops

The location of the shop varies according to the type of business and depends on the customs of the customers, such as their convenience in shopping and their durability in the region. The volume of trade in smaller units is affected by the location of chain stores, all kinds of stores and supermarkets (which act as magnets). These larger units should be located in a place that attracts the customer after passing the number of possible stores. The location of the shops should be selected based on the maximum trading potential. They also need to be viewed from as large an angle as possible.

The shape of the front of the shop, its signboard (integrated) and the system against protection against bad weather attract customers. The value of the shops located at the corner of the street is 30% more than the shops in the row. Each shop will have its own showcase (for example, a shoe shop window is different from a butcher and a jewelry store).

Furniture and interior design of commercial spaces

In department stores or shopping malls, the placement of equipment plays a major role in circulation. For this reason, the appropriate method of placing the transverse devices of the passage corridors is given here. The minimum passage width for one person between the shelves is 60 cm, but for the main corridors at least 1.90 meters and for the sub corridors at least 1.30 meters is enough.

Considering that one of the primary goals of designing a business center is to create a happy and uplifting environment that is always interesting to see, in this regard, the use of murals, sculptures, arboriculture, fountains, type of space paving, lights, graphic designs, paintings, ambient face lighting, how to arrange showcases and their lighting and creating focused lights for specific areas of open and semi-open void figures and billboards, pause spaces, lounges and seat of clients, shops and outdoor lobbies. The building (floor, ceiling, and walls), entrances and exits of the complex and even the music played in the complex can help to create an attractive and relaxing atmosphere.

2.4.4.3 Lighting in Business Centers

The appearance of the complex at night, both in terms of building and outdoor space, should be carefully studied, because in the centers that work during the night, a large amount of night shopping is done. In some places, light has a functional and safety role, such as car parks, parking lots, docks, etc. As a result, the correct choice of lighting fixtures, in addition to safety, also contributes to the beauty of the complex.

In general, ceiling lighting is required when designing business centers with large dimensions. Of course, daylight must enter the space in a controlled manner, so when designing the center with skylights, attention should be paid to the attractiveness of the population and the creation of interesting spaces for the public. Measures were taken to reduce the high height of such spaces, which sometimes reach up to 15 meters. Among the things that can be done, it must be mentioned that the use of large paintings hanging from the surface under skylights, large advertising screens, the use of waterfalls and sculptures, and so on.

In principle, when designing skylights, you should not use common forms and design all spaces as glass grids, but for example, you can use the design forms of old markets, which include four arches with perforated skylights. Of course, this does not mean imitating the previous forms, but this action should be done inspired by old patterns and by new technology, and in the end, aesthetic and functional solutions should be achieved.

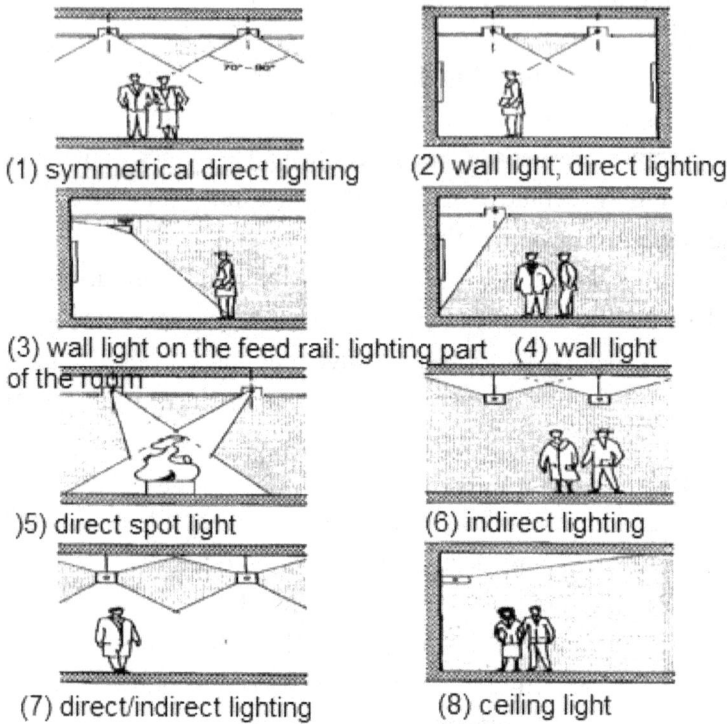

(1) symmetrical direct lighting

(2) wall light; direct lighting

(3) wall light on the feed rail: lighting part of the room

(4) wall light

)5) direct spot light

(6) indirect lighting

(7) direct/indirect lighting

(8) ceiling light

Figure 3.4

With the paging system, this system is completed in harmony with the bright paths and acoustic design, the indicators of which are proper sound return, sound absorption, sound reflection, sound level distribution and a suitable place to consider the location of the speakers.

Since shops should have different uses, they should have maximum flexibility. For this purpose, it is better to predict a changeable system in creating false ceilings and partition walls: for example, partition walls, prediction a changeable system. For example, the partition walls of commercial units should be of non-load-bearing style so that they can be moved, if necessary.

2.4.4.4 Columns and Skeletons in Business Centers

The dimensions of the columns determine the division of the spaces. The recommended skeleton for large stores is between 7.30-9 meters and in smaller stores is between 5.30-6 meters.

Depth of Commercial Building

In commercial centers, if the service facility is in the basement or on a surface other than the ground floor, the entire ground floor can be allocated for sale. In this case, the depth of the building is less than the case where the service facilities are located on the ground floor. Therefore, the depth varies between 44 and 54 meters depending on the existing conditions.

2.4.4.5 Circulation in Business Centers

Circulation of a business unit is of special importance and causes no movement interference in a business unit. In general, the delivery route, customer and employee input should be separated from each other. Sometimes it happens that due to the impossibility of a suitable space, the entrance of goods and employees are separated from each other, in which case a suitable locker room for employees (0.4 to 0.5 square meters per person) should be provided.

Horizontal circulation of customers is through vertical ways circuits to the places of vertical circulation. Escalators and elevators that form a vertical circulation must be beautiful and clearly visible so that they can attract customers to visit other floors. It should be noted that if the stairs in a business center are also used as emergency exit stairs, then the distance between the two stairs should not be more than 50 meters. Stairs and elevators can be placed in different ways relative to each other, but what is certain is that the main stairs, whether escalators, ordinary or elevators, should be located where they are visible from the entrance and are preferably located in the central part.

Vertical communication in stores and business centers is done by stairs, elevators or escalators. The number and width of stairs is determined based on the number of entrance and exit doors. If the stairs in a large business center are also used as emergency exit stairs, then the distance between two adjacent stairs should not be more than 50 meters. One of the fire safety regulations in the UK stipulates that in large buildings, the space must be divided into sections with a maximum volume of 7080 cubic meters (About 1700-1500 square meters with a height of 4 to 5) and each section has a separate escape staircase, this has caused the number of stairs in such stores to increase and instead, reduces the width of the stairs. Stairs and elevators can be placed in different ways relative to each other, but what is certain is that the main stairs, including public stairs and escalators and elevators, should be located where they are visible from the entrance.

2.4.4.6 Showcases in Business Centers

In stores, the showcase and the way it is placed and its arrangement has an effective role in sales. Therefore, proper design of the showcase and maximum use of storefronts to display the goods is very important. How to light the showcases is one of the things that should be considered because the depth of the showcase and the material of the back wall and the angle that this wall has with the horizontal surface of the window, can affect the reflection of light and vision.

The view of each showcase determines its value. Showcases with proper light and without glare can have an effective advertising effect.

Stunning showcases, reflective screens, and deep, dark showcases significantly reduce the value of the goods on offer.

Sweating and freezing of very cold showcases can be eliminated as follows:

1. For showcases attached to the shop with hot air flow over the entire area, if necessary by the ventilator for closed or very high and low showcases approximately 1.3 for glass.

2. Heating of glass by complex hot air pipes, electric infrared radiators, etc. under glass at intervals of 100-150 mm.

3. Insulated glass by trapping a layer of air, less air loss that prevents transpiration and freezing.

Regarding the use of advertising, some experts believe that tenants in shopping malls should follow a standardized design and marking for business units. This theory, given that every store, depending on the product it offers, must use a particular advertisement, which seems to be somewhat extreme, is 100% unpleasant control and creates uniformity, but reasonable control is necessary.

In general, posters, boards, etc. should be prevented from being pasted on showcases.

Waterfall in Business Centers

In general, the use of water, whether in the form of waterfalls or in the form of shallow or deep waterfalls, gives a lot of beauty to the space. Two factors, plant and water, which are the main and important factors of natural beauty and human artifacts soften, especially in the area of large buildings.

Fountains, which are sometimes one of the pillars of the basic design of Iranian architecture, have even overshadowed the location of the building. Many important buildings that were placed on the canals or springs, including Kashan Fin Garden and Golshan Tabas Garden, etc. can be mentioned. Controlling the movement of water and purifying it to control micro-organisms and aquatic magnifying glass that cause turbidity and discoloration of water is one of the important issues and should be addressed during the design of fountains inside the business center and pumping should be designed in such a way that it is not raised in the architecture of the waterfall.

Green Space in Business Centers

The use of plants indoors and outdoors always helps to soften the space and expand. The use of green space and plants in the interior spaces of the business center makes the spaces pleasant. Plants are easily supplied and grown through ceiling lighting due to their interest in overhead lighting. In this context, it attempts have been made to prevent the entry of sunlight in various ways, but in some spaces, special facilities must be used to compensate for the lack or absence of the sun. One of the most important features is the use of lamps that have the same function and solar energy by creating light with a spectrum of sunlight.

Ventilation in Business Centers

Business centers are one of the most crowded spaces that should be paid much attention to their ventilation to avoid creating an unpleasant and non-breathable environment and by creating environmental comfort for customers and businesses can increase the prosperity of business and attract customers. Because in a comfortable environment, they are more willing to spend time and buy necessities. In general, the problem of ventilation should be considered and solved in the early stages of design. Since otherwise in the next stages it can incur heavy costs for business centers.

Parking in Business Centers

In the business centers that were previously built, car parking facilities either did not exist at all or were available to a small extent. However, today, due to the importance of this issue and the fact that consumers usually go to these centers to buy by car, a suitable space for parking cars is also provided. And according to the existing standards, for each 20 m^2 of commercial space, 3.5 to 5.25 parking spaces with 3 to 4 times of change are required. In general, in large commercial complexes, passenger, pedestrian and freight access should be separated from each other. Basically, the shortest route, which is better to be covered, is considered for customers. In this regard, bus stations and subways should be at most 200 meters away from stores to better establish facilities.

2.4.5 Restaurants

In restaurants, the design of dining tables plays a major role. Tables can be arranged simply or diagonally. In a simple layout, a wide aisle is required for service between each row of tables.

The required area for the table top includes corridors of $1/42 \times 2/20$ square meters.

The required space for each guest along with the space in front of the doors is approximately 1.5 meters.

The space between two tables can be filled with small tables 65 to 70 cm.

Columns should be placed between a group of tables or in the corners of tables.

In the diagonal layout of the tables, the required area for each table includes 3.31 square meters of corridors and the required area for the guest is 0.83 square meters. The columns should be placed in the corners between the tables. If necessary, the service should be placed in front of the tables. Folding tables next to folding chairs are very simple and comfortable to store and save space.

The distance between the tables is approximately 1.3 meters.

The benches are only 43 cm high and 10 cm away from the tables, which makes it easy to enter from behind. If the rooms are 4 or 5 meters high and have light on both sides, the depth can be 15 to 20 meters. Tables can be grouped in rows or in two rows in the middle depending on the depth of the hall. In any case, the space used is not very different.

Figure 3.5

Figure 3.6

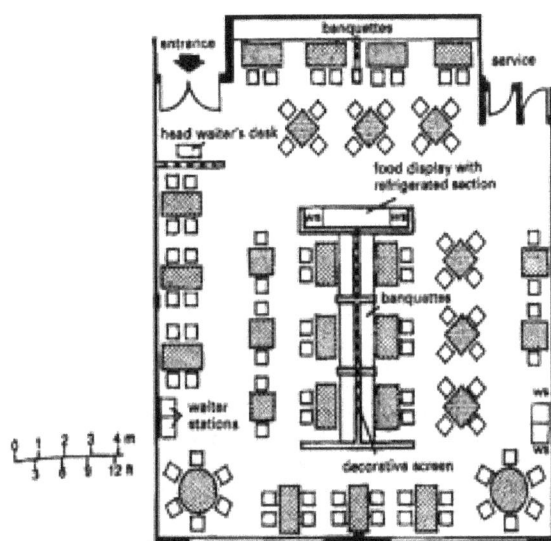

(1) Traditional restaurant: 110 seats

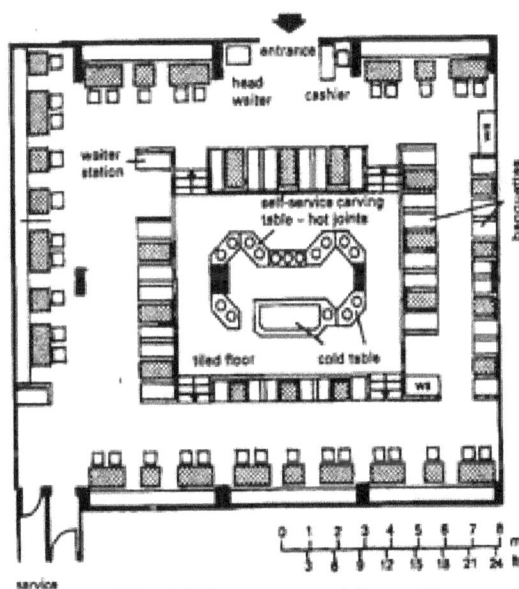

(2) restaurant with 124 seats with self-service table

Figure 3.7

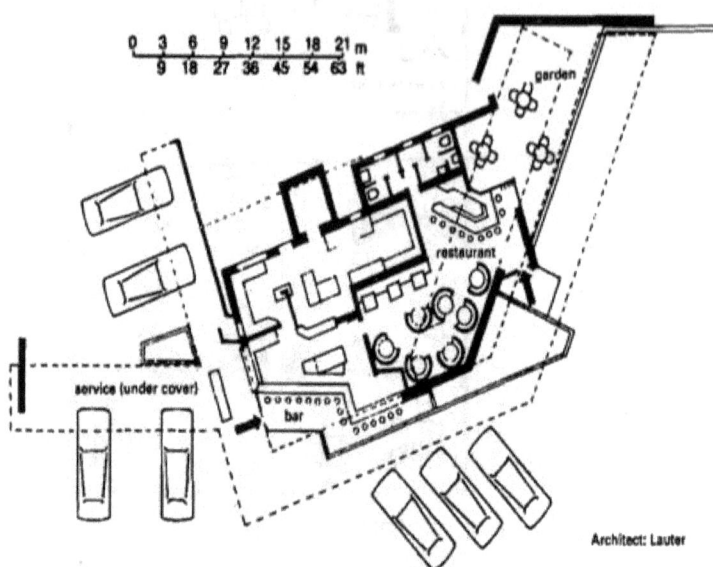

0 3 6 9 12 15 18 21 m
9 18 27 36 45 54 63 ft

garden

restaurant

service (under cover)

bar

Architect: Lauter

(3) Drive-in. A restaurant with special auto service, Claifornia

Figure 3.8

Chapter 3:

Biophilic architecture

3.1 Literature Review

In explaining the word biophilic, it should be said that this word comes from the word biophilia. The word biophilia consists of two components, bio and filia. The word bio is a prefix used at the beginning of nouns, adjectives and adverbs related to living things or human life. The word filia is a charm and a positive feeling that people have towards the habits, activities and all things in nature around us. As a result, biophilia is the same positive feeling of human beings towards living beings.

The word biophilia has Greek origins, meaning "love of life or living systems." Wilson uses the term to describe the innate connection of man with other living species (Kahen, 1997, p. 9).

Used in 1964 to describe the psychological tendency to be obsessed with all living things. The word is literally a name that entered Webster's dictionary in 1979 and means the innate human ability to communicate and be intimately related to other types of life and creatures in nature. The word biophilia also literally means love of life and creatures or systems of life. The concept of biophilia was also introduced by Harvard researchers and naturalists. The theory of biophilia (city in the garden) first by Smith. She. Wilson was born in 1993 (Sharifi and Azar Pira, 2014). Biophilic planning expresses the creative combination of green urban design with the participation of outdoor life, protection and recovery of green infrastructure from neighborhoods to biological areas and even higher levels (Ziari et al., (2015: 33) Biophilic urban design also means that cities more than Focusing solely on urban beautification, the pursuit of capital from the direct and indirect benefits of using nature as an indicator of functional and conceptual design that can be brought into the daily lives of urban dwellers.Figure 1-2 shows the benefits of biophilic urban planning.

Used in 1964 to describe the psychological tendency to be obsessed with all living things. The word is literally a name that entered Webster's dictionary in 1979 and means the innate human ability to communicate and be intimately related to other types of life and creatures in nature. The word biophilia also literally means love of life and creatures or systems of life. The concept of biophilia was also introduced by Harvard researchers and naturalists. The theory of biophilia (city in the garden) first by Smith. She. Wilson was born in 1993 (Sharifi and Azar Pira, 2014). Biophilic planning expresses the creative combination of green urban design with the participation of outdoor life, protection and recovery of green infrastructure from neighborhoods to biological areas and even higher levels (Ziari et al., (2015: 33) Biophilic urban design also means that cities more than Focusing only on urban beautification, pursuing capital gains from the direct and indirect benefits of using nature as an indicator of functional and conceptual design that can be brought into the daily lives of urban dwellers. Figure 1-2 shows the benefits of biophilic urban planning.

Lehmann (2010, 2005 & 2009) outlines 15 principles of biophilic urban planning guidelines, including:

1. Weather; 2. Renewable energy to prevent CO2 emissions; 3. City without waste and garbage; .4 water; 5. Landscape, garden and urban biodiversity; 6. Sustainable transportation and good public space: crowded and multi-center cities; 7. Local and sustainable materials with low energy consumption; 8. Compaction and reinforcement of existing sections;

9. Green buildings and sections, using passive design principles; 10. Programs to create vibrant, healthy communities with mixed use; 11. Local food supply chain; 12. Cultural heritage, identity and sense of place; 13. Urban leadership and governance and adoption of best practices; 14. Education, research and awareness; 15. Strategies for cities in developed countries.

Biophilic urban planning is used in different scales from single building to blocks and neighborhood units and scales such as the city and offers different forms, forms and executive proposals suitable for each scale. Examples of the application of the induction of biophilic concepts in the case of urban rivers, which are subsets of the neighborhood and city unit scales, can be the opening of some or all closed water streams, streams and drainage of running water, which ultimately causes Improving water quality, creating favorable conditions for river aquatic animals and connecting urban green paths for pedestrians and cyclists are mentioned. A number of cities, such as Zurich, Germany, and Seattle, USA, have done similar projects. In an executive example in the city of Seattle, by returning a part of the Ravina River to the city level, a very beautiful and magnificent natural space has been created by reviving the native vegetation next to the residential area. The Ravina River, which flowed underground in the early 1990s, was returned to the city by a private company (Pinkham, 2000). City Scale Recently, with the role of green infrastructure becoming more prominent, many cities are making increasing efforts to improve ecological and hydrological systems at the regional and environmental levels. Most of these cities have rebuilt and protected rivers in the hope of establishing a physical connection with them (Beatley, 2005: 120-127). For example, new efforts are being made to revitalize the Los Angeles

River. The Los Angeles River, which now looks more like a water canal than a natural river, flows through almost every part of the city and has real potential to improve the quality of life of thousands of residents around the river through 239 green space projects (Anderson, 2007). Many biophilic urban planning programs offer exciting opportunities to design communities and cities around the world and increase the number of policymakers who have been able to gain popular support for urban nature enhancement programs (Beatley et al.)., 2009: 19). For example, the city of Seoul in South Korea, in a dramatic move, removed the eight-square-kilometer stretch of highway that opened the Chuangi Chuan River, which was below the highway, to the city. The project, carried out by a former Seoul mayor who later became the 17th president of South Korea, shows that projects to support and develop the foundations of the biophilic city also have political benefits. In addition to environmental benefits, the project also had economic and cultural benefits (Revkin, 2009).

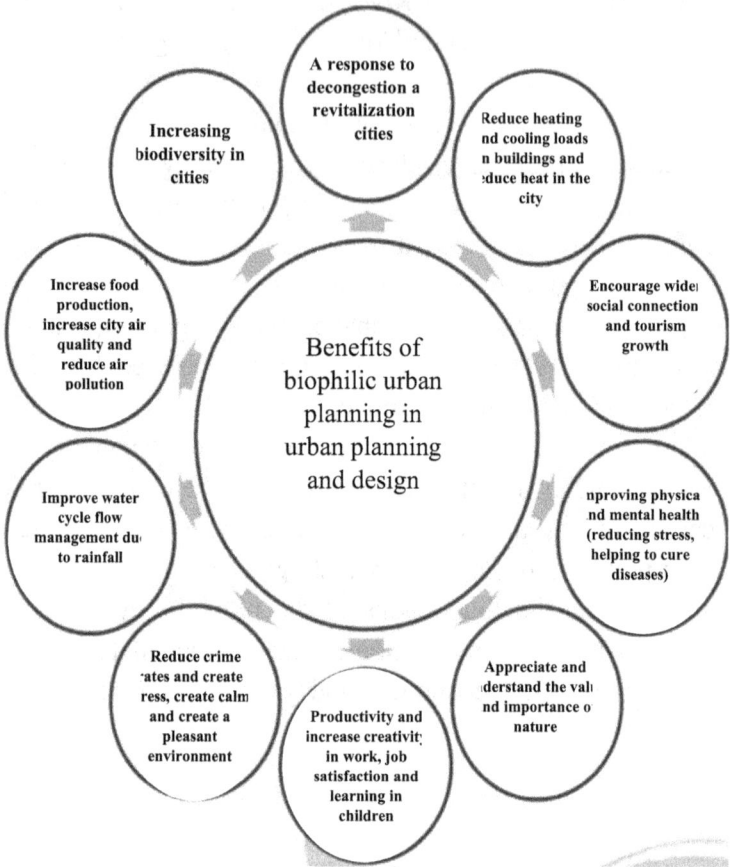

A response to
decongestion a
revitalization
cities

Increasing
biodiversity in
cities

Reduce heating
nd cooling loads
n buildings and
:duce heat in the
city

Increase food
production,
increase city air
quality and
reduce air
pollution

Benefits of
biophilic urban
planning in
urban planning
and design

Encourage widei
social connection
and tourism
growth

Improve water
cycle flow
management du
to rainfall

nproving physica
nd mental health
(reducing stress,
helping to cure
diseases)

Reduce crime
·ates and create
ress, create calm
and create a
pleasant
environment

Productivity and
increase creativit:
in work, job
satisfaction and
learning in
children

Appreciate and
iderstand the vali
nd importance o
nature

Figure 3.1 .Benefits of biophilic urbanization. Source: (Ziari
et al., 2015: 14; Mir Gholami et al., 2016).

3.2 Theoretical Foundations

3.1.1 The theory of biophilia

Biophilia is the innate human desire to connect with and join
nature. However, in the process of human modernization, this
innate desire is in a critical state, as a result of which the
mental and physical health of human beings has been
damaged. The idea of biophilia stems from an understanding

of human evolution. More than 99% of the history of human evolution has been developed in response to and adapted to nature in a completely natural process, not artificial or man-made, but what we usually admire today is historically Compared to the whole course of human evolution, it is related to the end of history. Large-scale food production in the last 12,000 years, the invention of cities 6,000 years ago, the mass production of products and goods 400 years ago, and electrical technology has only been formed since the 6th century AD. The human body, mind, and emotions evolved in a biocentric way, not by engineering or the world of technology. (Kellert, and Calabrese, 2015). This is exactly what mankind seems to have forgotten.

3.1.2 Biophilic design

Biophilic design is, at a glance, the recognition of man's innate need to connect with nature, along with sustainability and global design strategies for creating environments that can enhance the quality of life. Professor Claret sees biophilic design as a new model of green architecture that promises to reconnect humans with nature. In general, biophilic design is a careful attempt to understand the inherent human need for solidarity and connection with the natural world and its impact on the design and construction of suitable living environments. This is relatively easy to understand, but it is extremely difficult to achieve nonetheless. Because there are limitations to a full understanding of human biology and the various aspects of its institution and character to connect with the natural world, and because there are other limitations that make it difficult for us to convey these concepts in the design of buildings and environments. Makes. (Barkhordari, Nikpoor Nikpoor, 2015)

Unfortunately, modern (new) technology and engineering advances have led people to believe that natural and inherited genes cannot limit them and can even adapt to them and rise to the top. This belief has strengthened humanity's notion of escaping the domination of the systems of life by human progress and the growth of civilization in a way that has the ability to fundamentally change and transfer the natural world. This dangerous illusion has created an architecture that results in extreme density of buildings, shrinkage and collapse of the surrounding natural environment, and separation of people from natural systems and processes. The dominant pattern in the design of modern (new) constructions is that the building has become a consumer of unstable resources and energy. This type of architecture spreads air and water pollution, pervades climate change, destroys the rights of future generations, creates unhealthy indoor conditions, creates alienation from nature, and causes homelessness. Biophilic design is an attempt to bridge the gap between modern (modern) architecture and the human need to connect with the natural world. Biophilic design is an innovative approach that emphasizes the importance of maintaining, enhancing, and restoring the beneficial experience of using nature in the built environment.

3.1.3 Definition of biophilic design

Biophilic design is, at a glance, recognizing the innate human need to connect with nature, along with sustainability and global design strategies for creating environments that can enhance the quality of life (Julie Stewart, 2006). Professor Claret sees biophilic design as a new model of green architecture that promises to reconnect humans with nature. In general, biophilic design is a careful attempt to understand the inherent human need for solidarity and connection with the natural world and its impact on the design and construction of suitable living environments. This is relatively easy to understand, but it is nevertheless extremely difficult to achieve, as there are limitations to a full understanding of human biology and the various aspects of the institution and its character for connection to the natural world, as well as other limitations. Because of our inability to convey these concepts in the design of buildings and environments, it makes work difficult for us (Stephen R. Kellert, 2008).

3.1.4 The concept of biophilic design

The concept of biophilic design Biophilic design is actually design and construction according to nature in mind. Of course, biophilic design does not mean greening our buildings with grass and vegetation and simply enhancing their attractiveness and beauty by using trees and shrubs. Rather, the subject of our discussion is much higher than this, and about the place of humanity in nature, as well as the place and place of the natural world in human society, a space where confrontation, respect and valuation of communication can occur at all levels and appear as a norm. Exception.

3.1.5 The origin of the idea of biophilic design

The idea of biophilic design began when the knowledge of the evolution of the human body and mind and its connection to the sensory and precious worlds increased, something that continued to the point for human health, productivity, emotions, intellectual and mental development and even human mental health. A crisis arrived and became vital. The necessity of this issue in modern (contemporary) era is obvious in cities due to large-scale agriculture, industry, artificial materials, various engineering, electronic world, etc. Human beings can evolve by reacting according to natural conditions and stimuli. Conditions and stimuli such as: (sunlight, air, water, plants, animals, landscape and canvas) are essential for puberty, functional development, and ultimately human life.

3.1.6 Biophilic design goals

Biophilic design goals We are a society that is constantly changing and moving, and we always create a lot of stress for ourselves, our children, co-workers and our neighbors, and cause an imbalance in our body that leads us to diseases and It takes a long time to heal. There are many observations that show that nature-inspired environments help us to be less stressed and able to control it, and we can also provide productivity, creativity, job satisfaction, an environment conducive to children's mental and physical development. ... and finally, it can give us a part of the peace of mind we desire. The following are some of the most important things that biophilic design has a positive effect on:

- Physical and mental health
- Creativity, attention and learning in children
- Satisfaction with the environment
- Productivity and creativity at work, job satisfaction, avoiding unnecessary absences from work.
- Neighborhood relations and interaction in cities.
- Create peace of mind and reduce stress
- Appreciate and understand the value and importance of nature.

3.1.7 Professions involved in biophilic design

As mentioned, biophilic design is an interdisciplinary discipline and involves many different disciplines, including: architects, natural scientists, sociologists, health professionals, psychologists, climatologists, ecologists, biologists, urban planners, and It includes urban planners, developers and all those who suggest how we can create not only sustainability but also a satisfying and new society that is in harmony with nature.

3.1.8 Principles and benefits of biophilic design
The challenge of biophilic design is to show the shortcomings of current buildings and the urban landscape in such a way that it can develop a new framework for creating a desirable sense of the presence of nature in environmental buildings. Biophilic design also seeks to create a suitable habitat for humans as a biological organism in modern environmental buildings, in a way that increases health, spiritual enrichment and a sense of happiness in humans. (Kellert, and Calabrese, 2015; 152)

3.1.9 Principles of biophilic design
The successful performance of biophilic design depends on adhering to its basic principles. These principles state the underlying conditions for an effective biophilic design. These principles can be enumerated as follows:

- Biophilic design requires frequent and continuously enhanced communication with nature.
- Biophilic design focuses on human adaptation to nature, which has promoted human health and satisfaction during human evolution.
- Biophilic design encourages emotional dependence on specific environments or places.
- Biophilic design promotes positive action and reaction between people and nature. In a way that encourages the development of a sense of solidarity and responsibility between human societies and nature.
- Biophilic design encourages integrated and two-way solutions for architecture. In other words, the architecture that strengthens the relationship between

man and nature, as well as meeting the needs of modern man, is the goal of biophilic design.

Figure 3.2. An integrated design with a two-way connection between man and nature

3.1.10 Benefits of biophilic design

Successful performance of biophilic design will have a wide range of positive physical, psychological and behavioral effects.

- Physical achievements such as: increasing body health, lowering blood pressure, reducing the symptoms of diseases.
- Extensive psychological results such as: increase satisfaction, reduce stress and anxiety, increase problem-solving power and increase creativity.
- Positive behavioral effects such as: improving collective abilities and teamwork, raising the level of focus, improving social relationships and reducing violence.

3.1.11 The main patterns of biophilic planning and design

3.1.11.1 Biomorphic patterns and shapes
In general, biomorphic is a style in design in which the object is shaped and shaped in such a way that it represents an organic and living being or creature (Bahmani, 2009: 22).

3.1.11.2 Green space-based development and public transportation
Crowds around a public transportation station and a park (or a bio-functional environment) Environmental and pollutant reducing) with biological function at the neighborhood level (Betley, Newman and Boyer, 2009: 15).

3.1.11.3 Visual connection with nature
Attention to the elements of nature, living systems and natural processes is emphasized in this model (Terrapin Bright Green, 2014).

3.1.11.4 Non-visual connection with nature
This pattern, through auditory, tactile, olfactory, and taste stimuli, provides the context for voluntary and positive attention to nature, living systems, or natural processes (Ryan et al, 2014: 77).

3.1.11.5 Irregular and rhythmic sensory stimuli
This model considers random, variable, and transient relationships with nature (Alvarsson et al, 2010: 25).

3.1.11.6 Adjacent to water
In this model, an attempt is made to provide the field of watching, drinking and touching water and to provide conditions to increase the connection with the natural environment (Browning, Ryan and Clancy, 2014: 15).

3.1.11.7 Connection with natural systems

An environment that communicates well with natural systems alerts people to environmental changes. The purpose of linking to the pattern of natural systems is to increase awareness of natural features (Ryan et al, 2014: 77).

3.1.11.8 Connection with natural materials (stone, wood, etc.)

In this model, natural materials and elements provide the local environment with minimal processing. The purpose of it Creating a sense of spatial belonging (www.greenroofs.com, 12/6/2015).

3.1.11.9 Complexity and simplicity

Complexity and simplicity include rich sensory information that emphasizes spatial hierarchy (Salingaros, 2012: 14).

3.1.11.10 Landscape

A landscape has an implicit and subjective meaning. The landscape model is rooted in research on visual and spatial tastes as well as cultural anthropology, evolutionary psychology, and architectural analysis. The purpose of the vision model is to provide visually appropriate conditions to individuals (Batley, 2011: 17).

3.1.11.11 Mysterious environment

Research has shown that exposing a person to a mysterious and predictable environment that requires revelation triggers a pleasurable reaction in the human brain (Herzog and Bryce, 2007: 51).

3.1.12 Solutions for using biophilic design

Biophilic design includes various strategies that should be selected according to the project performance, economic conditions, ecology and culture of the project site. The most important point in biophilic design is that this design should not look like an accessory or decorative member to the building. Rather, it should be used as an integrated method in the building so that each of the strategies reinforces the other and a perfectly coordinated result is achieved. (Kellert, and Calabrese, 2015: 86)

There are three categories of feelings and experiences towards nature in biophilic design that will reflect the basic principles of this design. To create each of these psychological experiences, there are several components and design strategies that are described below. (Kellert, and Calabrese, 2015: 87)

Direct experience of the presence of nature: This experience and feeling is the result of a real connection with natural components in environmental buildings such as animals, plants, water, etc.

- The experience of the indirect presence of nature: This experience and feeling goes back to an image of nature, or the development of some natural patterns, ie inspiration from forms and shapes in nature, as well as the direct use of natural forms.
- Feeling and psychological experience of space and place: This experience and feeling to certain features that an environmental space can induce and thus improve a person's physical and mental health; It is related to creating a sense of expectation, curiosity, mobility, and so on.

Table.1. Classification of components and strategies of biophilic design according to various experiences of communication with nature

Direct experience of the presence of nature	Experience the indirect presence of nature	Psychic feeling and experience of space and place
Light	Pictures of nature	Waiting and security
Air	Natural materials	Organized complexity
Water	Natural color	Integration of components with the whole
plants	Simulated light and weather	Transition spaces
Animals	Forms and shapes corresponding to nature	Dynamics and routing
weather	Calling nature	Cultural and ecological relationship with the environment
Natural ecosystem	Information richness	
Fire	Life, change, the passage of time	
	Natural geometry	
	Biomimicry	

3.1.13   Components and strategies related to biophilic design

3.1.13.1 Direct experience of the presence of nature

3.1.13.1.1 Light

The presence of natural light is essential for human health. Humans have long been able to distinguish between seasons and day and night based on the location of the sun using light. The presence of light creates a feeling of comfort and awareness of environmental conditions. In design, deceptive shapes can be created in the environment through creative interaction with light and shadows. Glass walls, atriums, paints and light-reflecting materials can be used to deepen the presence of light in the space. This pleasant feeling that the light is moving can be created through the contrast between the light and dark parts as well as the changes of daylight during the day.

Figure 3.3. Create charm through playing with light

3.1.13.1.2 Air

Access to natural ventilation is essential for human comfort and efficiency. Natural ventilation can be created through changes in flow, temperature, humidity and air pressure. These conditions can be met by access to the outside environment through simple solutions such as pop-ups or new engineering techniques. (Kellert, and Calabrese, 2015: 92)

3.1.13.1.3 Water

Water is essential in human life and can have positive effects such as reducing stress and increasing productivity. By using other properties of water such as sound, movement and touch, the attractiveness of the presence of water in the environment can be increased. There are many strategies for connecting with water in the design of environmental buildings such as fountains, aquariums, artificial lakes. The presence of water in the environment is more pleasing when it is clean, moving and with the use of other properties mentioned above.

Figure Error! No text of specified style in document.**4. Presence of water in the environmental building (Kashan Fin Garden)**

3.1.13.1.4 Plants

One of the most successful experiences of the direct presence of nature in buildings is the planting of plants, especially flowering plants. The presence of plants reduces stress, contributes to physical health and improves comfort. Of course, it should be noted that the use of plants in a protected or alone and limited way will have fewer positive effects. It is very important that the plants planted in buildings and the environment should be part of the native plants of the region and compatible with the ecology of that region. (Kellert, and Calabrese, 2015: 93)

3.1.13.1.5 Animals

An inseparable experience of man throughout the history of his evolution is the presence of animals and living next to them. Useful communication with animals can be achieved through green roofs, gardens, aquariums and bird nests, as well as more technological methods such as films, binoculars. Communication with animals in a limited and highly protected way has little positive effect, resulting in effective communication that includes a variety of animal species and relies on local natives. (Kellert, and Heerwagen, and Mador, **2008**)

3.1.13.1.6 Weather

History has shown that climate change is essential for human beings. This is met by simple design strategies such as casement windows, porches and gardens. (Barkhordari, Nikpoor Nikpoor, 2015)

Natural ecosystems

Ecosystems include car plants, animals, natural rocks, and natural forms. Humans have been present in ecosystems since the beginning of creation and then in their evolution, and therefore prefer even the simplest natural ecosystems to their artificial ones. Examples of design strategies such as the construction of an artificial lake, green roof and all-grassed areas can be mentioned (Figure 5). Planting plants. (Barkhordari, Nikpoor Nikpoor, 2015)

3.1.13.1.7 Fire

One of man's greatest achievements was fire. Because it leads man to restrained energy, and this ability is beyond the capabilities of animals. Design strategies for using fire are the use of fireplaces and fire stations in general. But in a simulated way, designs can be made using the creative use of light, color, mobility, and heat-transfer materials. (Kellert, and Heerwagen, and Mador, 2008)

3.1.13.2 Experience the indirect presence of nature

3.1.13.2.1 Pictures of nature

The use of images of nature, including plants, animals, geological forms, etc., can be emotionally and mentally effective for humans. Representing nature using photographs, films, paintings, sculptures or any simulation method can be used in design. Limited or individual use of nature images will have little effect on the audience, so these images should be used frequently, with a specific theme and specific to the culture and environment of the same area in the design.

3.1.13.2.2 Natural materials

Usually, as much as artificial materials look exactly like their natural counterparts, natural materials are a priority for humans. Because a kind of dynamism due to the passage of time is seen in natural materials, even if it is a rock material. 3 For the interior design of buildings can be used materials that include wood, stone, wool, leather, etc. The belief that matters is derived from nature leaves a sense of wonder, including that people will be less stressed in these places. (LBC, 2014)

Figure 3.5. Use of wood as a natural material in the building.

natural colors

Colors have been important to humans since ancient times and have been used to identify paths, find food, and so on. Appropriate use of colors in biophilic design should be such that they represent only the extinct such as the color of rocks, soil and various plants. The use of bright colors should be cautiously combined with other colors to reflect nature scenes such as sunsets, rainbows, flowers. Excessive use of highly contrasting colors and synthetic colors should be avoided. (Kellert, and Heerwagen, and Mador, 2008)

Figure 3.6. Use natural colors

3.1.13.2.3 Simulated natural light and weather

With the advancement of technology in the construction of buildings, it became possible to simulate indoor natural light and processed air. These days, in companies and factories, most activities are sedentary, and these conditions can weaken a person physically and mentally. Artificial light can be such that the occupants of the building feel the spirit and movement of natural light. The processed air is simulated with features that induce the quality of natural ventilation by circulating air and creating the right humidity and pressure. (Kellert, and Calabrese, 2015: 95)

Figure 3.7. Natural light simulation

3.1.13.2.4 Forms and shapes corresponding to nature

A desirable feeling is formed in man from the forms and forms taken from nature. These forms can be unusual and unique. For example, columns in the shape of leaves. Building views such as plants, fabrics of the same sex and design as animals. Forms and shapes that correspond to nature can make a living space in a way that reminds the qualities and dynamics of living spaces. (Kellert, and Calabrese, 2015: 97)

Figure 3.8. Special use of shapes found in nature

3.1.13.2.5 Calling nature

The feeling of satisfaction from the connection with nature can be created in human beings with imaginative and fantasy drawings, but also inspired by nature. Such drawings do not occur exactly in nature, but they still use the principles that we encounter in nature. The Sydney Opera House, for example, is reminiscent of the features of several beach oysters. Notre Dame's glass window gives the viewer the feeling of a rose. The skyline of some cities looks like a vertical heterogeneity of forests. None of these exist exactly in nature, but it is the principles and characteristics of the natural world that have shaped them. (Kellert, and Calabrese, 2015: 98)

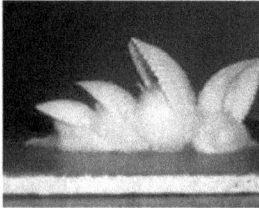

Figure 3.9. Sydney Opera House reminiscent of oysters

Information richness

Much has been said about the diversity of the natural world. Nature is known as the richest source of information that man can encounter. Man is also inherently interested in being in spaces that offer him many opportunities and options at the same time. As a result, environments that provide information to individuals in a complex but coherent manner are of interest to biophilic design.

Figure 3.10. The Bird's Nest is a complex transmitter of information, and the stadium is inspired by it.

3.1.13.2.6 Life, change, the passage of time

Nature is constantly changing. Life in particular reflects the forces of growth and aging. People react positively to this rust over time. This tendency becomes more desirable for people when the integrity and strength of the building is also seen in this passage of time. Changes and changes in time in the design can be presented to the audience using materials that naturally show the effects of aging, passage of time and erosion. (Kellert, and Calabrese, 2015: 98)

3.1.13.2.7 Natural geometry

Natural geometry refers to the mathematical properties that are commonly seen in the shapes of nature. This geometry often includes curved forms instead of the artificial one, which is more rigid and sharp. Shapes that are constantly repeated and create different patterns. Other prominent natural geometries include the golden ratio and the Fibonacci sequence. (Kellert, and Calabrese, 2015: 99)

Biomimicry

Solutions can be found in the structures of nature for the problems of architecture and construction of human societies. These include the ability to control the climate of termite nests, spider web resistance, and the ability to trap heat by the hair of some animals. (Kellert, and Heerwagen, and Mador, 2008)

Using technology, we can extract and use features of this non-human nature that directly have positive results on human life. Traits that arouse human astonishment at the creativity and initiative of other living things and the natural world in general. (Kellert, and Calabrese, 2015: 101)

Figure 3.11. Create a vertical garden with patterns like tree branches

3.1.14 Biophilic importance

In traditional architecture, the building can be covered with plants to create a green building. But in biophilic architecture such a thing cannot happen, in this architecture must interpret the form of a large process and have many objective and subjective parameters. Green building is also a confusing term in biophilic architecture. A green building is a structure that can be shaped using renovation processes, while biophilic architecture is involved in the negative effects of climate and improves human physical and mental comfort to create a healthy life (Minke, 2001). Unfortunately, modern technology and engineering advances have led people to believe that natural and inherited genes cannot limit them and can even overtake them. This belief has strengthened the notion of humanity to escape the domination of the systems of life by human progress and the growth of civilization in a way that has the ability to fundamentally change and transmit the natural world. This dangerous illusion has created an architecture that results in the extreme density of buildings, the shrinkage and collapse of the surrounding natural environment, and the separation of people from natural systems and processes. The dominant pattern in the design of modern constructions is that the building has become a consumer of unsustainable resources and energy. This type of architecture spreads air and water pollution, pervades climate change, destroys the rights of future generations, creates unhealthy indoor conditions, increases alienation from nature, and it causes displacement growth. Biophilic design is an attempt to bridge the gap between modern architecture and the human need to connect with the natural world. Biophilic design is an innovative approach that emphasizes the importance of maintenance, enhancing the restoration of the beneficial experience of using nature in the built environment (stewart-pollack, 2006).

Biophilic architectural criteria

- Appreciate and understand the value and importance of nature.
  - Use forms of logic with nature
- Use of natural materials
- Use of natural components in environmental buildings such as animals, plants, water
- Creates peace of mind and reduces stress
  - Cultural and ecological relationship with the environment
  - Dynamic space and readable routing
  - Balance the environment with human auditory, tactile, olfactory and taste stimuli
- Neighborhood, interaction and commuting in cities
  - Optimal environmental access
  - Balance of population density
  - Spatial hierarchy
- Productivity and creativity
  - Evolutionary physical environment
  - Using natural elements
  - Increase communication with the natural environment
- Satisfaction with the environment
  - Create a favorable landscape
  - Creating the desired quality outside the building
  - Creating the desired quality of the interior of the building
- Creativity, attention and learning in children
  - Combining building and nature
  - Create change and movement in the outdoor environment
  - Create change and movement in the indoor environment
- Physical and mental health
  - provide security
  - Outdoor quality
  - Interior quality
- Calling nature
  - Green space development
  - Utilizing nature outside the building
  - Using nature inside the building

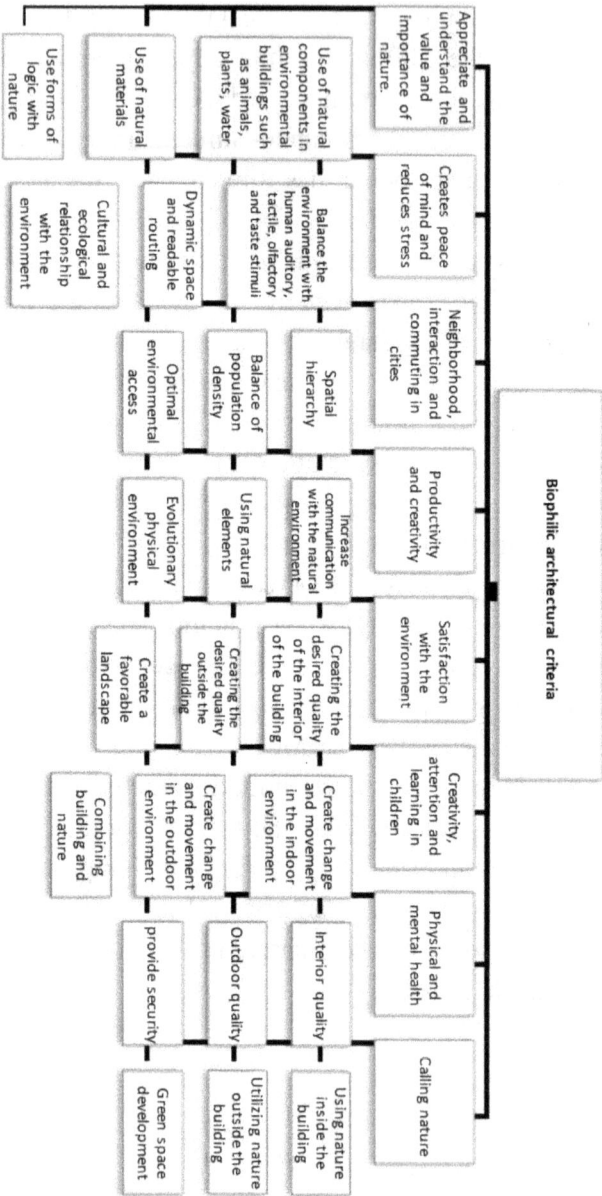

Physical criteria of bionic architecture

3.2 Analysis of interior and exterior design examples

With a glance at successful tourism projects in the world, we may be able to introduce new dimensions. Therefore, in this section, we will review some examples of these projects.

3.2.1 Bora Bora Hotel

The Bora Bora Hotel is located in the Tahiti region of South Africa, and was discovered by Spanish sailors in the 16th and 17th centuries under the direction of Captain Anthony Bongani Willy. The expedition was accompanied by Spanish sailors along with sailors from the Netherlands and Portugal.

3.2.1.1 History

After exploring the area, large groups of English and French traveled there from 1767; The island has been an official French colony since 1789. The island was finally colonized by Spain in 180 AD, and the country officially gained independence in 1984.

Eventually, after many ups and downs, 115 small and large islands were formed in the form of the Tahiti archipelago; The archipelago was divided into 5 provinces (states). The five provinces are Marcosas, Tamota, Gambir, Astral, and the Algerian community. The Algerian community was later renamed the Algerian community.

Tahiti is part of this part and Bora Bora area is located in the heart of the archipelago. The Bora Bora Hotel is located at the tip of the Ratite Cape; A place that has a perfect and very beautiful view of the ocean and rocks. The beautiful view of the volcanic mountains with the cloudy sky next to Mount Utama is very beautiful - Otmavo in the local language means mountain of birds.

3.2.1.2 Bora bora Hotel Design Concept

The main idea and concept of the design of Bora Bora tourist entertainment complex is based on 15 groups of "Poli Niza". Poli Niza is actually a type of chemical moon from the hexane group, which when called in a special way is called Namuli Niza.

The summer houses of this tourist complex are connected to the complexes and the beach through corridors. The extraordinary charm of this project is in the special order that governs the summer houses.

Figure 3.12: Bora Bora Hotel

The concept has continued in the choice of materials for the summer houses of Bora Bora Hotel and has tried to lose the sense of old merchants with a nostalgic view. The designer of the hotel summer houses with this look of bamboo and bamboo, which is reminiscent of ships, boats, etc .; Has used Tasmanian oak in the construction of walls and ceilings and floors. In the interior design beautifully placed all the facilities of the hotel. Most of the materials used in summer houses are red cedar wood. The highly climbing American Douglas Fire plant on cast iron roofs has given these houses a special look.

Inside these houses, canoe pedals and fishing hooks have been used for decoration.

3.2.1.3 Check out the cottages

3.2.1.3.1 internal space

These houses are branched and have a full view of the ocean. The spacious bedroom with large bathroom is worth noting. The living rooms have a small patio, which is designed like a pond and a lagoon. Some units have a sun terrace, all of which are located on the beach. The cooling and heating system of houses is air conditioning.

3.2.1.3.2 Placement of summer houses on the water

Bora Bora Hotel summer houses are in the form of 15 complexes; Which are placed side by side in a circle. The space in the middle of them creates a form that creates a beautiful pond and swamp.

Figure 3.13. Placement of summer houses on the water

The ocean blue color of these ponds is stunning. The water around these summer houses is coral, which has its own charm. Next to the terrace of these houses, there is a staircase that leads directly to the water under the houses. There is a shower next to all the stairs. The strip shape of these houses has given a special beauty to the complex, the lack of full view overlooking other houses, the soothing sound of the ocean water, the feeling of seeing and touching the ocean in this way has created a lot of peace for tourists.

3.2.1.4 Forest cottages

These houses are located in tropical forests, which are connected by a short path to the complex of summer houses on the water. The difference between this group of houses and the previous group is that each house has its own pool. The facilities of these houses are the same as the previous part, but in the part of the sun terrace, a larger area is dedicated to this space; The infrastructure of these houses is about 82 square meters.

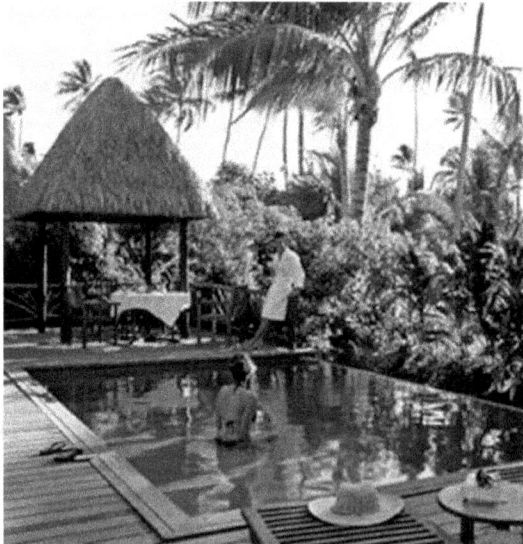

Figure 3.14. Forest cottages

3.2.1.4.1 Check house plans

Rooms at this hotel are generally one-bedroom, two-bedroom and suite with pool. In one-bedroom rooms, according to the purpose of the design, most of the infrastructure of the house is dedicated to the living room and sun terrace. Because the most important thing in the location of these houses is the experience of living for a short time near the ocean.

Because basically, the type of tourism of this complex has been ecotourism, and in this group of complexes, the architectural design of the units should have the most benefit and visibility to the outside as much as possible. In other words, the maximum amount of transparency.

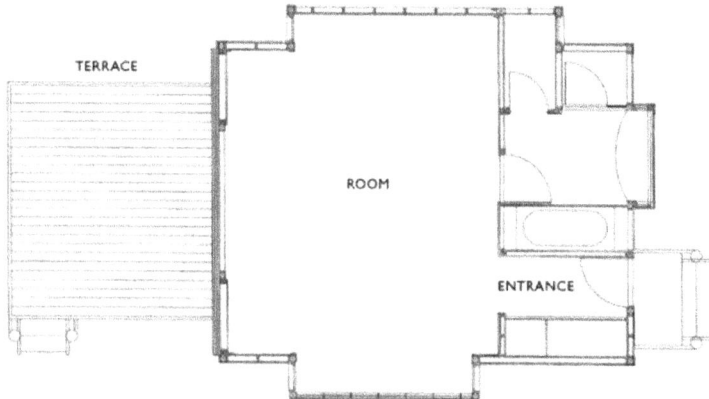

Figure 3.15. Check house plans

In two-bedroom rooms, the plan is the same as one-bedroom; But there is a big difference in the plan of the suites that have a pool. In these units, a very large terrace is considered, due to the existence of a swimming pool in the unit.

In the corner of the terrace is a pergola and Barbie Q, the bedrooms have a full view of the pool and the view behind it.

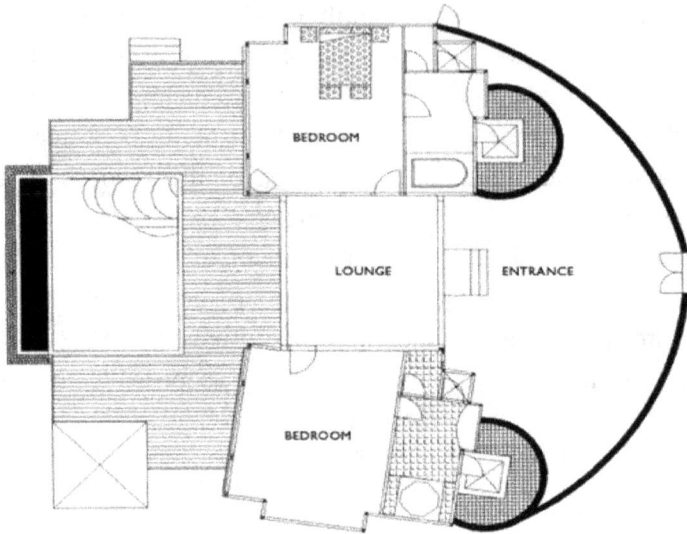

Figure 3.16. House plans

3.2.1.5 Food and catering at Bora Bora Complex

Breakfast, lunch and dinner are served at Matira Restaurant. With a large terrace overlooking the ocean. During the gentle breeze, the restaurant places its tables and chairs, which are made of bark, in this area and the reception is done outdoors. There is an evening meal with dessert and tea if needed. Of course, all catering services can be done privately in the rooms during certain hours.

3.2.1.6 Other special activities at Bora Bora Complex

3.2.1.6.1 Show

Live music is played three times a week according to the previous schedule. There is also a local show once a week. The live dance and singing program is also a nightly program each week. Along with the program, there are fast food sandwiches for eating. Presenting the native arts of a country can make the helplessness of a good work of entertainment a lasting effect. In the show part of this complex, an attempt has been made to do this point efficiently.

3.2.1.6.2 Store

The shops and stores of this hotel mostly offer local handicrafts. In these shops, there are books introducing the country's tourist attractions and local clothes for display and sale.

3.2.1.6.3 Jewelry

This unique store, which is the only official jewelry and pearl store in the whole island, has unique ornaments specially decorated with black pearls. The important point is that the black pearl industry is the first industry in this country and tourism is in the second place. contract.

3.2.1.6.4 Entertainment

The center provides services in two groups; The first is reading and the second is fun and entertainment. In the second part, there are all kinds of TVs, movie players, CDs, DVDs, etc. There are bingo tables, lotto, dominoes, jack wards, etc. for fun. It is also possible to see the beautiful areas of the country through television. In this section, wireless internet is provided to applicants for free.

3.2.1.6.5 Sport

Two standard tennis courts with night play are located in the center of the recreation area. The grounds have a platform for a limited number of spectators. In these fields, sports equipment such as rackets, balls, etc. are provided to the players on loan.

3.2.1.6.6 Air tour

This tour, which is done by helicopter, has a unique charm that allows you to see the island from the air. In this tour, it is possible to visit the adjacent small and large islands. The experience of air recreation is one of the things that is welcomed by many tourists in the world today.

3.2.1.6.7 Water fun

Bora Bora Hotel has many facilities for providing water sports and recreational services; Sports such as swimming, diving, fishing, jet skiing and more. The azure waters of the Pacific Ocean are a good place for such winds. In this section, we take a very brief look at these sports.

3.2.1.6.8 Diving and diving

Some of the best divers in the area are working at the Bora Bora Hotel to offer a very exciting diving sport. The hotel diving club is located in a beautiful location next to the beach and the hotel's dense forest.

There is scuba diving to more or less depths, with advanced equipment and facilities. Many parts have been identified in the coral reefs of the ocean to visit; Which take groups there. Of course, these areas are explored depending on the number of skills and experience of the people.

3.2.1.6.9 Pleasure boating

Bora Bora Hotel has organized various half-day and one-day tours in this area. Special 15-meter yachts with many facilities are built to travel a few kilometers in the heart of the ocean. Special three-day sea tours are also done with these boats, which are not without merit. During these recreational programs it is possible to go rowing with rowing boats.

3.2.1.6.10 Swim

The Bora Bora Hotel is surrounded by ocean water on three sides; The white sands of the beach excite all people who love the beach and swimming in the water to enjoy this pleasant atmosphere.

The design of the beach in front of the hotel is such that it is possible to use the beach until the evening when it gets dark. This is the maximum use of solar energy from good architectural design standards.

3.2.1.6.11 Jet ski

Next to the Matira restaurant is a jet ski station that runs around the island; And places that cannot be easily reached with rowing boats. Today, this recreational sport is one of the most popular water sports in the world.

3.2.1.6.12 Water Journey

For people who are not allowed to dive due to various reasons or restrictions; Cruise has been replaced so that they cannot miss the beauty of the ocean. Guests can use underwater hats and glass-bottomed boats to see underwater and walk under shallow water. Many fish are found in coral reefs.

3.2.1.6.13 Beach picnic

Guests and tourists can travel and walk a few tens of meters away from the big waves of the ocean. The 40-kilometer coastal route on the island passes through exotic forest areas. However, surfing on land such as the sea and ocean can be interesting and memorable.

3.2.1.7 Bora Bora Hotel Analysis

Bora Bora Hotel is located on Tiny Island; This small island is about 8 km long and 4 km wide. The island is located northwest of Tahiti. The high and volcanic mountains of Otamo overlook the island. About 80 beach resorts have been seen in this entertainment complex, places such as summer houses, entertainment center, beach, restaurant and so on.

The architect and designer of the complex has built the spaces based on the use of local and traditional materials of the island. In the construction of these places, the use of old construction details of houses has been highly emphasized and considered by the designer. This has resulted in a visual matching in addition to inducing and displaying the island's native houses. As the project is done entirely on a human scale and this issue has a great impact on the rapid connection of tourists with the complex.

In the design of houses, public furniture, leisure centers and equipment of Bora Bora Hotel complex, local handicrafts and handicrafts using local wood have been used a lot. Basically, the Bora Bora Hotel Complex has placed a lot of emphasis on preserving the old feel of the island; But modern facilities and services are well placed in this ventricle.

The interior design and amenities of the complex are in line with the highest global standards of tourism, which provides a sense of peace, comfort and security for tourists. There are also a number of suites on the water based on the monetary concept; All of these houses and villas are designed based on full view of the ocean. Of course, the constant breeze that enters these houses creates its own pleasant atmosphere. In designing the landscape and environment of this complex, vegetation of forest and tropical areas has been used. In the back of these houses, there are service, support and accommodation parts for servants.

In this complex, all the necessary facilities for tourists have been considered and built and paid according to the standards and principles of tourism at the world level. These facilities include a variety of water sports (swimming, diving, jet skiing, boating, etc.), ground sports (basketball, tennis, volleyball, etc.), restaurants, shops, medical services and other essential facilities.

The land area of this hotel is 16 hectares and a total of 80 summer houses are located on this site. Complete water recreation facilities, a view of all the houses to the ocean, excellent sports fields have made this recreation complex one of the ten natural recreation complexes in the world; And perhaps the collection of the best small houses in the world in this complex. One of the main topics in modern tourism, which is defined as ecotourism; It is fully implemented in the Vera Bora Hotel complex. There are two axes based on services, design and facilities in this type of tourism: the first is the short-term experience of living in the heart of real nature. The second is to create the least amount of environmental degradation in the region.

Figure 3.17. Hotel Borbora

3.2.2 Lost City Palace

In the center of the volcanic valleys along the Pilansberg Mountains, a mysterious and gigantic complex rises from the ground. This complex is so great from afar that it looks more like a mirage. This complex is undoubtedly one of the greatest architectural wonders of the African continent.

The designer of the Soul Kreuzner collection, far from the hustle and bustle of the native people and relying on the highlights of the legend of the lost city, added a fully equipped and entertaining entertainment section to the complex.

Figure 3.18. Lost City Palace

Last City is a large and luxurious hotel located in the southern part of Africa. In a city known as Sun City; The complex is located 120 km from Johannesburg. This is a large five-star world-class tourist and accommodation center, and the complex has been named the best hotel in the world by Lodging Hospitality Magazine.

3.2.2.1 The Legend of the Lost City

The Legend of the Lost City Palace is a mythical tale from ancient Africa that is mostly fictional. The Lost Palace has been a legendary place where there have been abundant dense forests, rocky forests, large waterfalls, rivers, lakes, and massive catchments. Inside the palace, the motifs on the paintings, bedding, sculptures have been various and wonderful colors. The legend states that the lost city was the cradle of civilization and the symbol of Africa in the past.

Fantastic and strange things have been said about the palace of the lost city. The splendor, glory, grandeur and magical grandeur of the palace is the most that can be deduced from this legend. Eventually the palace collapsed in a devastating earthquake and was destroyed forever.

3.2.2.2 Introduction of Last City Complex

The complex is located in an area of about 25 km; It has 350 very luxurious rooms, 21 special suites. In this complex, in general, there are 6 restaurants, an Olympic-sized swimming pool, an amusement water park, an 8-square-kilometer lake, two golf courses (with a 13-hole field and an 18-hole field), a game and entertainment center, and so on.

The facilities in this complex have been installed without any shortcomings and in this respect, it is perhaps one of the most complete residential and tourist recreation centers in the world. In this section, more complex analysis is done. Due to its size, a full review of the center is out of the question.

3.2.2.3 Services in Last City Complex

There are a variety of restaurants and eateries in the luxurious Last City complex. In fact, maybe every person with their own taste, can find their favorite food among the available restaurants. A number of restaurants serve foreign food. One of the most famous of these restaurants is the Palazzo restaurant. This restaurant with a terrace overlooking the lake is a place to eat European food, especially Italian.

The remarkable thing about the hotel is that the strong management of the hotel has made breakfast, lunch, dinner and supper to be taken to the room or suite of tourists at the request of tourists. A beautiful central courtyard called Crystal Court with very tall windows and Ghadi has a fascinating view of golf courses, dense forests and rivers. This section is for serving traditional and local dishes. Task Bar restaurant also has a special atmosphere in serving delicious dinners. The appetizing table and desserts after the local food of this restaurant are famous. A very interesting point is the presence of 6 pairs of ivory in the central foyer of this restaurant, which weighs about two tons.

3.2.2.4 Complex vegetation

Around the forest complex with an area of 25 hectares has been built, which is completely artificial. In this forest, about 1600,000 types of trees, shrubs, bushes and plants in the form of 3200 plant species have been planted; A real forest of native plants of the African continent.

Figure 3.19. Complex vegetation

These forests are planted in three types according to the classification of rainforest tree species:

A. Very tall tropical trees called umbrella or shade trees, with an average height of 40 meters.

B- Normal and medium trees that have a height of 2 to 6 meters

C - green plants and shrubs with a maximum height of 1 meter.

In this vast artificial forest, artificial lake, river, waterfall, pond and several reservoirs have been designed and built. The design style is all organic and so harmoniously designed that few people think that all these spaces are artificial.

3.2.2.5 entertainment facilities

In this complex, there is one of the largest adult entertainment complexes in the world. The special and unique design of the children's playground is remarkable. In the entertainment section, all kinds of game tables, two golf courses with world standards - one 13 holes and the other 18 holes - with a completely unique design, sports fields are recreational facilities. These are complexes.

Amusement Park Last City Amusement Park, with an area of 55,000 hectares, is one of the third wildlife parks in Africa. In the recreational wildlife forest of this complex live about 10 000 native wild animals of the region. Among them, there are about 300 rhinos, hippos and protected giraffes. It is possible to explore with four-wheeled motorcycles or cars in this park called forest tour. There are balloon flights over the park; The artificial lake of this complex, which has large waves with advanced devices, has made the experience by the sea and the beach possible.

Figure3.20. Leisure facilities of the hotel

3.2.2.6 Recreational sports

Due to the large number of tourists in this complex, a lot of sports fields have been provided in two dimensions, type and number, which are mentioned only in this section. Some sports have ten pitches next to each other, which means that the number of people who can play at the same time will be much higher. Recreational sports include golf, bowling, horseback riding, squash, trampoline, water sports, tennis, water tube riding, swimming, volleyball, surfing, and more.

There are a variety of sports in bodybuilding and fitness. These include gymnastics, standard swimming pool, four-season pool, children's swimming pool, massage parlor, sauna, Jacuzzi, yoga salon and more. The following are some examples of specific recreational sports.

3.2.2.6.1 Archery

It is a fun sport that is approved as an ancient sport in Africa; It has many charms. This indigenous sport, which is considered as a martial art in that country, is presented in this complex with modern equipment. These include cameras, rails, introductory training by masters who are skilled in how to use bows and arrows.

3.2.2.6.2 Shooting with a gun

For those who enjoy real shooting for fun shooting; Last City Recreation Complex has a shooting range. The target on this land is the clay bird pigeons - in the shape of a circular disk. There are experienced trainers to ensure safety and more fun.

3.2.2.6.3 Excursion tour with elephants

The experience of old wildlife can be a very exciting and different pastime. The elephant tour includes a visit to the true, natural and original location of the elephants on the

African continent. The elephants' habitat is located in a place called Elephant Valley. They return to the hotel around.

3.2.2.6.4 Recreational motorcycle riding

These recreational four-wheeled motors have a very simple operation. In addition, driving with them is very enjoyable, comfortable and exciting. These motors are practically capable of moving on a variety of hard and uneven objects; This makes it possible for tourists to visit inaccessible places. Places such as the main habitat of wild animals such as rhinos, giraffes and so on. The leaders of this group must be very experienced people.

3.2.2.6 Large palace pool

This massive swimming pool is located in the main entrance - see the map of Last City Recreation Center. This large pool is decorated with many mosaics and sculptures, in fact, this pool makes the heat of the region less effective. There are two well-equipped restaurants next to the pool. The first is a bar buffet that serves fast food and ready meals. The second is the snack cafeteria, which sells cocktails and desserts, drinks and ice cream.

3.2.2.7 Review of the architecture of Last City Complex

The architectural issues related to the Lacit City Tourism Accommodation Complex are reminiscent of interesting points that reflect the thinking in the tourism industry. The basis of the design and concept of the design is based on a mythical legend of a palace in the lost city, which was briefly described. But turning a legend with a cultural and indigenous infrastructure into a tourist and recreational space seems like a huge and difficult task.

Creating a castle-like appearance with tall and symmetrical turrets is a symbol of greatness and stability. Maintaining symmetry in form, shape and volume is one of the important architectural indicators of the complex and a part of design rules and frameworks. The creation of large lakes on either side of the central building is important for a reason:

Symmetry and proportion, by creating the preservation of the text of symmetry on the sides of the central building.

Adjusting the humidity and ambient temperature, the presence of two large pools on the north and south sides of the building reduces the hot air temperature in the area, and increases the ambient humidity.

Therefore, the designer has been able to use the element of water in the form of a pool or lake, in addition to beauty, to give a better feeling to the people inside the site.

Basically, the cultural infrastructure of Africa is a manifestation of a very royal and luxurious life due to the constant poverty and lack of facilities. According to statistics, expensive cars and very luxurious houses are an integral part of the African people today.

In the legend of the lost palace, in accordance with this case, there has been a lot of talk about its splendor, glory and grandeur. Up to 60 to 70 meters of building turrets confirm this. In general, perfect symmetry is one of the basics of luxury design, which can be clearly seen in this complex. Inside the collection, warm and spicy colors are often used, which look at the background of African chromatography.

One of the wonders of construction in Last City Complex is that, for the construction of two golf courses in the complex, an artificial lake, a swimming pool, etc., about 600,000 trucks of soil have been moved to create a suitable topography. Moving this amount of soil is enough to build at least 40 football or polo fields.

Figure 3.21. Architecture of Last City Complex

During the construction of the complex, 5,000 workers were permanently employed. This huge project, which is among the recreational complexes of the city, has been built with the help of the latest technology and prefabricated parts in just 30 months.

However, this really huge project, which is valid according to world standards and classes, is unique in its kind; And every year a large number of enthusiastic tourists from all over the world travel to this region.

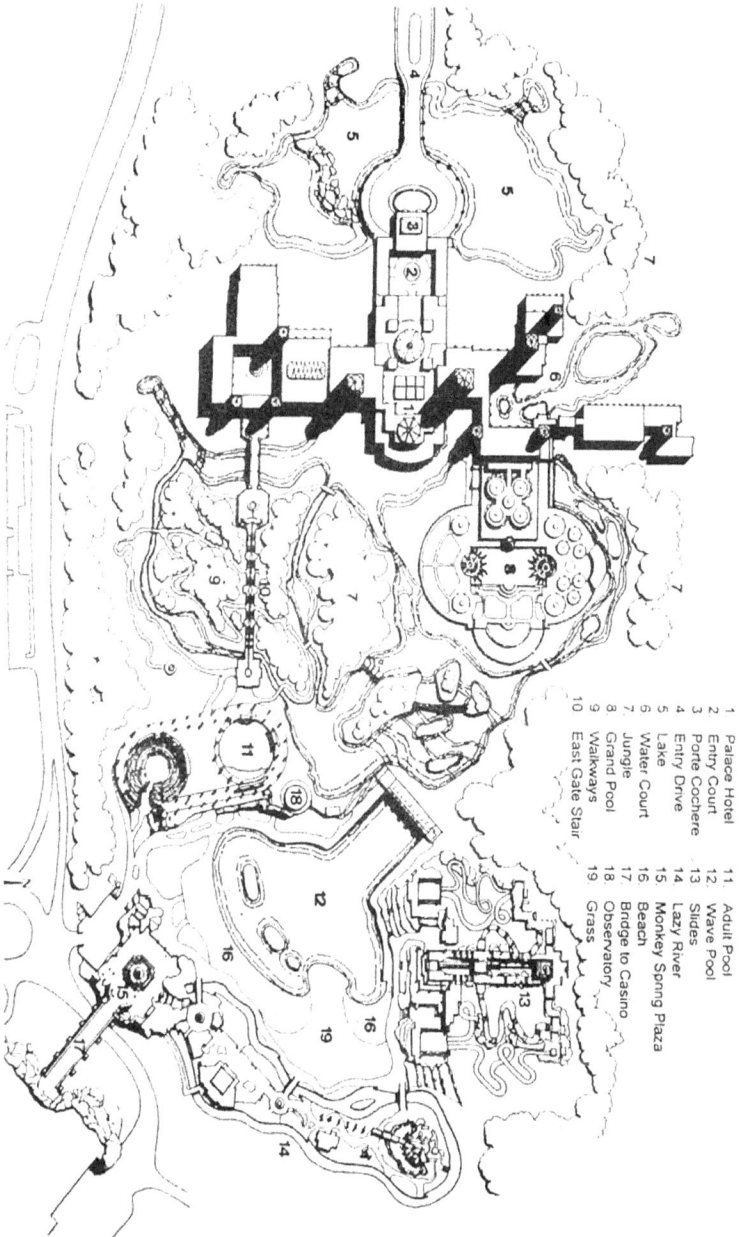

1   Palace Hotel
2   Entry Court
3   Porte Cochere
4   Entry Drive
5   Lake
6   Water Court
7   Jungle
8   Grand Pool
9   Walkways
10   East Gate Stair

11   Adult Pool
12   Wave Pool
13   Slides
14   Lazy River
15   Monkey Spring Plaza
16   Beach
17   Bridge to Casino
18   Observatory
19   Grass

Figure.22. Architectural plan of Last City Complex

3.2.3 Ainak Lake Residential Cultural and Recreation Center

The city of Rasht, as the center of the province, which attracts both the population and covers many surrounding cities and villages, is facing such a problem and shortage due to the tourist attraction of the region. For this reason, an attempt has been made to build a large complex of cultural, sports, tourist and recreational spaces such as this complex to address these shortcomings.

The location of the Ainak Lake project is the plan of the Rasht community. Lake Aynak is a green space or a tourist-hospitality use.

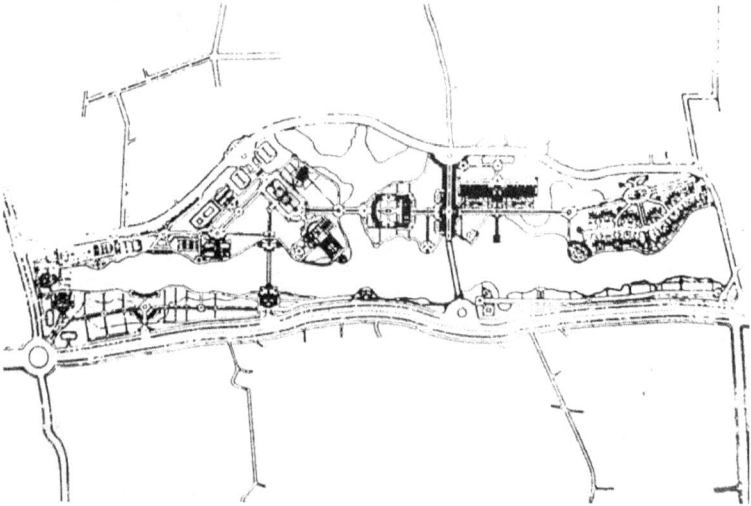

Figure 3.23. Ainak Lake Residential Cultural and Recreation Center

This area is a suitable bed. Ainak Lake is a large reservoir in the west of Rasht city and at the beginning of Rasht-Fooman Road, which is one of the most suitable places for a region due to its pristine and beautiful nature and potential economic and environmental facilities. It is fun.

Unfortunately, this lake is declining due to the intervention of uninformed human beings and the invasion of urban machine life. A recreational-tourism complex can be a step towards revitalizing the lake in addition to meeting some of the city's needs in this area.

3.2.3.1 The main pillars of the center design

It is divided into three main parts:

1- Knowing the condition of the design bed
2- Plan program goals
3- Architecture
In the first part, the current situation and the possibilities and limitations of the region and the needs of Rasht are studied. In the second part, while dealing with the characteristics of traditional and indigenous architecture of the region, the general objectives of the design and design criteria and criteria are discussed, based on which, the proposed solutions are evaluated and the optimal solution is proposed. The third part, which is architectural design, examines the proposed design from the point of view of design pattern, architecture and implementation.

The main goal of the project is to create a calm environment, with various functions, related to nature, for people to spend their leisure time. In Iran, nature and natural resources have always attracted people and a center for recreation and relaxation, among which gardens have been the most important, therefore, this complex is designed in the form of a park or large garden, each of which is the axis It has been formed according to the principles observed in Iranian gardens and Islamic gardening.

A continuous, coordinated and orderly collection of water and plant architecture forms the main backbone of the Iranian garden. Gardening in Islamic architecture is a wonderful phenomenon of harmony and harmony, which is a harmonious and orderly perception, located at the intersection of passages that include life and greenery in their area.

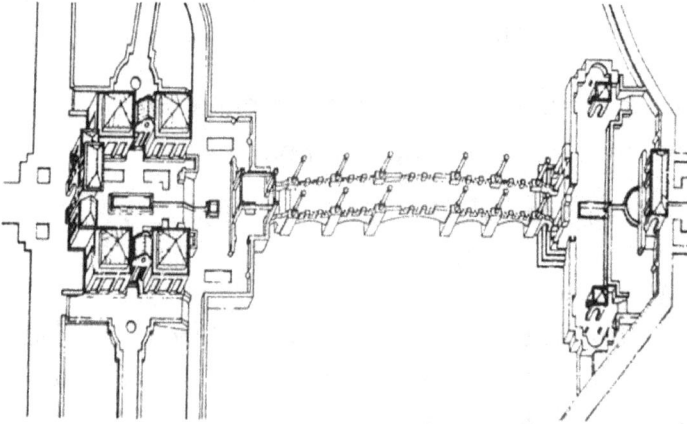

Figure 3.24. Design of Ainak Lake residential and cultural recreation center

3.2.3.2 Principles and benefits of the plan

Although Iranian gardens have special regional methods in terms of construction and have long been built in different ways according to the type of land and the amount of water, in terms of architecture and building elements and in terms of design patterns, style. They are the same. The main factors that make up the Iranian garden are: the enclosure of the garden - the existence of a water feature, etc. Among the famous Iranian gardens, we can name Eram Garden, Finn Garden, Behshahr Garden and Takht Garden.

Other issues in the design of spectacle collections are climatic factors. The climatic needs in this region are such that design without considering them is unprincipled and impossible. The most important issue in the design is the use of air flow and creating comfort against humidity and protection from rain. The principles observed in the design are as follows:

1- Dispersion of the complex, in order to maximize the use of air flow.

2- Proper orientation of the building, in order to penetrate the desired wind of the area.

3- Using covered corridors or open joints, in order to establish the relationship between buildings.

4- It has the use of sloping roofs for protection against rain.

5- Using double-walled walls to deal with moisture penetration.

6- Using a chair of such a stone, in order to prevent the infiltration of soil moisture.

In the last section, the design pattern and architecture of the design are examined.

3.2.3.3 Design concept

The main idea in the whole design is to create a major axis in the form of a sidewalk within the complex, as the main backbone of the design, which causes continuity and integration in the whole complex. Due to the importance of base movement at the level of the complex, it has been tried to combine this main pedestrian axis with open and semi-open spaces, squares, water features and platforms, etc. This movement is accompanied by diversity and continuity. Another principle in the design of the complex is the correct replacement of functions and building elements in a logical relationship with the pedestrian and wall axes and achieving a general order. The collection of glasses, due to its special formation, due to the shape of the lake, is in fact a wide collection that has been tried in each of its axes, as a part of the whole smaller order, based on the principles of Iranian gardening, public order in To be provided throughout the collection.

3.2.3.4 Introducing the center

The glasses collection with an area of approximately 41 hectares, consists of various uses with their own spaces, which are:

A- Cultural and religious spaces

B- Sports and recreational spaces

C- Tourist spaces

D. The north side of the lake, which is the boundary between the main road and Ainak Lake and is completely dedicated to green space and is designed as a park with recreational use.

3.23.5 Cultural and religious spaces

A- The cultural complex consists of three buildings:

1- Library, 2- Amphitheater, 3- Center for intellectual development of children and adolescents and in addition, it has a kindergarten and an open amphitheater on the lake shore.

B- Exhibition complex which includes exhibitions, museums, art education classes and outdoor exhibitions.

C- The mosque which has been formed as a religious indicator by using natural elements and by creating cultural spaces.

D- Flower Garden, which is designed in combination with the park space and includes four greenhouses and a central building, which is the central plant studies section, which includes the plant studies section of the offices and plant sales.

3.2.3.6 Sports and recreation spaces

A- Sports hall which is considered as an indoor according to the special climate of the region. This complex acts as a gymnasium with several halls.

B- A set of outdoor pools with the necessary equipment, which are formed next to each other.

C- Outdoor sports fields

D- Sailing club, as a sports-recreational space, provides the possibility of using the lake for sports and water recreation.

The restaurant, which is designed as a reception-welfare unit in combination with the park space and can add to the functional richness of the complex.

3.2.3.7 Tourist spaces

A. The guest house, which is actually a villa complex and consists of two main parts:

1- Residential spaces or villas.

2- Central space including service and reception areas.

B- Camping or multi-day camping place, which is designed as an extensive system (residential units around a main feeding route) in the heart of nature and residential units can be used in that tent.

C- A picnic or a one-day party place, as a recreational and recreational space that is designed inside the park.

3.2.4 Mirza Kuchak Khan Sports and Entertainment Complex

The purpose of selecting and proposing this plan is to commemorate the great name of the man of Gilan, next to his permanent tomb and to create a collection in his honor, and then to revive Suleiman Darab neighborhood and the need of the city. Kuchak Khan's tomb is located in the southern part of Rasht, in the old cemetery of Suleiman Darab neighborhood.

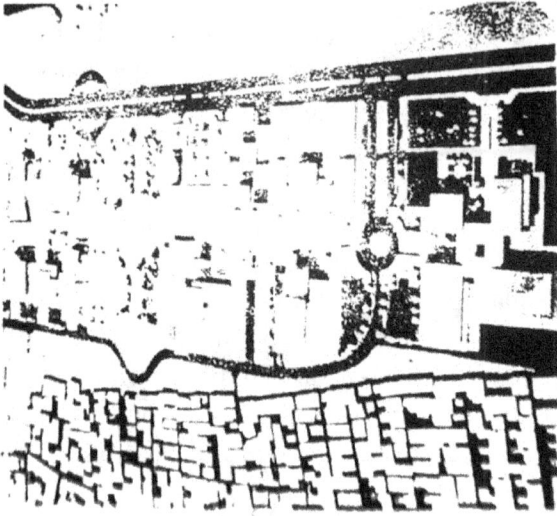

Figure 3.25. Mirza Kuchak Khan Sports and Entertainment Complex

The designed land with an area of approximately six hectares is located on the north side of the tomb. This land ends from the west to the main street, and from the east to the residential neighborhood. According to the studies conducted in the city and the comprehensive plan of Rasht city, which indicates the lack of quantity and quality of educational, sports-recreational, administrative and cultural uses, as well as the study in the neighborhood, the shortage of the mentioned users in the city and the studied neighborhood. Has been selected for a neighborhood center with cultural-educational-recreational-commercial and sports uses.

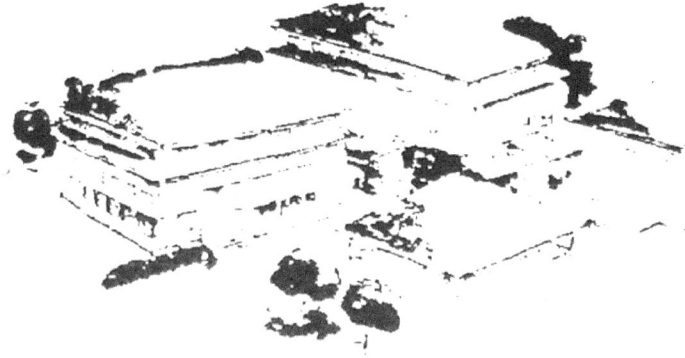

Figure 3.26. Mirza Kuchak Khan Sports and Entertainment Complex

3.2.4.1 The main areas of the collection

The plan includes spaces that are generally divided into two main areas of cultural and recreational services. According to the definition of domains and how to access them, the location of land uses has been done in such a way that everything in the domain is defined and has a logical relationship with the surrounding functions.

3.2.4.2 Cultural field

In the cultural field, due to the location of the small tomb of Khan, cultural and administrative buildings are located next to the tomb. Therefore, by creating an order and locating cultural buildings next to the order, it ends at Mirza's main monument. This part of the project includes spaces such as museum, library, office, amphitheater and music halls, handicraft workshops, office building of the complex and also the memorial building of the complex.

Office Building
Library

Exhibitions and
museums

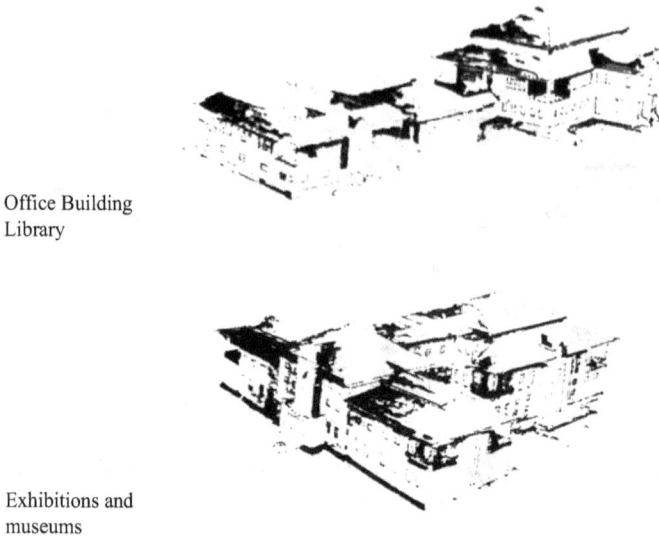

Figure 3.27 .The main areas of the collection

3.2.4.3 Recreational services

The recreational services area is designed for its public and of course crowded performance, a short distance from the tomb and like the cultural complex. This section includes: gyms, bazaars, amusement parks, cinemas, parking lots and kindergartens, in connection with the residential section and the whole complex (for staff). Rider access to the residential area is also possible from this part.

3.2.4.4 Specifications and design spaces

On the south side of the library complex is an exhibition of manuscripts and an office building. This complex consists of three interconnected buildings. The library is designed for public use throughout the city and the manuscript building is designed to hold valuable books and manuscripts in such a way that all its installation issues can be controlled. This center is located between the office building and the library, and in connection with these two buildings. The management of different parts is located in the office building, and the general administration of the building has been assigned to this part. The area around the mausoleum consists of old tombs and tombs of martyrs in which no construction facilities can be constructed.

Light elements such as columns can be used to join the tomb to the complex. Using traction cables, light roofed spaces can be created around the tomb so that the tomb is located along the main axes of the complex. Along the main axis of the pedestrian and the center of the cultural area, a square has been designed which is located in the center of the memorial building of the complex and has reached the highest height by an elevator and overlooks the whole complex. Around the square, spaces on two levels have been designed for relaxation and open exhibitions. To the east of the complex is a museum and a gallery of paintings and photographs that are connected by a bridge on the first and second floors.

The location of the school is located next to the residential area, on the south side of the complex. The school is designed in two floors and 14 classrooms. The cultural section is a collection consisting of three assembly and music halls, respectively, in the east of the main pedestrian row, the large hall for performing music concerts, and the western side of the small hall for performing local music and music education class. Next to these two halls is the Ershad office building. The design of this building is square and has three floors with space frame cover.

The cultural area has been separated from the recreational services area by a green space filter and a waterfront (park), in coordination. This area includes spaces - more and more crowded than the mentioned spaces. The cinema next to the bazaar is one of these places. The bazaar consists of 24 shops and a dining hall, the second floor of which is dedicated to a traditional teahouse. The cinema hall is designed for a capacity of 500 people. This capacity is considered according to the number of cinemas in the city and the needs of the neighborhood. Kindergarten is designed next to the park and parking lot and children's play space and residential area, so that the spaces are used to the maximum. The park and parking lot are integrated in such a way as to create a very favorable atmosphere for everyone.

On the ground floor (pilot) there is a parking lot and warehouses. On the upper floor there is a park and a waterfront and a number of shops.

Next to the main belt of the city - the end of the main pedestrian row located in the northern part of the land - is a sports complex. The purpose of designing this complex is to create a place for extracurricular youth activities in the region. This complex includes the entrance hall, indoor pool hall, indoor pool hall, volleyball, basketball and wrestling hall, office building on the first floor of the central part (hall) and Shatanraj club. The parking lot, which is sufficiently designed around the sports complex, prevents the spread of vehicles on the surrounding streets and facilitates access for customers.

Due to the low soil resistance of the area, the foundation of all buildings is of concrete strip type and also concrete columns are predicted. The roof covering is mainly made of space frame system and all its nodes, hot-dip galvanized (due to high humidity) by plate (hot-dip galvanizing and moisture insulation) with its own special details.

3.2.5 Recreational-cultural complex of Kerman revolution

Attention and optimal use of the remaining spaces within the city for the development of public spaces and urban parks can not only increase urban green space (which is necessary to balance the urban environment), but can improve the quality of life in cities. (Often introverted).

Kerman Municipality has tried to provide recreational spaces - including parks - in the city, to consider such goals: cultural and educational development, strengthening participation and social relations between people and also improving the quality of urban landscape to attract Tourism and revenue growth for the municipality.

The city of Kerman also has suitable capabilities in terms of natural features. The city is very diverse in terms of elevation, and in fact the mountain ranges on which the ancient castles of the city were built, are located in the middle of the city and therefore have given a special variety to the city morphologically.

Enqelab Recreation Complex with an area of about 4.5 hectares is one of the most important recreational-cultural centers of the large tourist recreation area of Kerman, which is in the final stages of construction and operation. This park is located next to the two routes of local access and urban access and has a special position to serve the citizens. Morphologically, it has many and varied elevations and heights that have created special conditions for landscaping the park. This area was the main cemetery of the city about 80 years ago and is the burial place of many celebrities, poets and scholars of Kerman. After the location of this area within the city limits and the cessation of the expansion of the cemetery and the prohibition of burial in it, this place gradually became an abandoned and abandoned space, and due to its informal constructions and also the large number of trees, It became defensive and conducive to concentrating anomalies and delinquency, and on the other hand it became a place for garbage accumulation, which was very annoying for the residents of the immediate area.

3.2.5.1 Introducing the collection

In the implementation of the plan of this complex, which includes three parks and the municipality implements it in a decision-making manner on the spot (and without anticipating the use of a special plan), three main goals have been considered.

The first goal in designing and implementing this park is to respect the historical and cultural elements of the complex in such a way that nothing in this park should overshadow these elements - either in terms of volume, volume or function.

The second main goal is to follow the natural forms and at least intervene in the natural state of the park, so that even the artificial elements added to the surface of the park are made using natural materials and are naturally inspired by natural volumes.

The third approach in organizing this park is to pay attention to the aspects of local tourism in this complex. For this purpose, suitable spaces have been considered in the mentioned complex with the focus on valuable cultural and historical elements. One of the most important of these spaces is the House of Persian Literature, which was formed around the tomb of the contemporary poet of Kerman, Ms. Hayati. Also, due to the multiplicity of historical elements and components discovered in the city of Kerman, a paleontological museum is being constructed in this park with the cooperation of the Kerman Cultural Heritage Organization. Dinosaur fossils discovered around the city of Kerman are the most important works intended for display in this museum.

In this collection, it seems that they generally have a good relationship with each other, and each of the elements has a specific and separated space so that the game, relaxation and cultural environment are completely separate. For example, dining in an open space has a spatial condition that provides the necessary comfort for users of this environment and is problematic for them in terms of audio-visual and safety.

3.2.5.2 Effective factors

The most important drawback of this project is the lack of proper studies and planning for the design of the park. However, the way the municipality deals with such a valuable complex, which can be of equal value to Bam Citadel, must be very careful. The fields of study required in the design of this collection should include four sections:

The first category is economic studies for items such as the cost or revenue of constructing such a complex, using the capabilities of the private sector or how to acquire existing land in the area of intervention for design. Ignoring any of these will make the job take too long.

The second category, studies can be dedicated to environmental studies and study of active natural ecosystems and their interaction with each other in urban space.

The third category is the beautification of the urban landscape in terms of urban planning.

The fourth category is the state of mental and physical needs of the people and the impact of this group on the health of society, which is very important from a social point of view.

In view of the above; First of all, the purpose of the design must be specified. In the next step, determining specific planning for studies and design in order to achieve the goals should be on the agenda. Finally, the effective determining factors in the design must be identified. Fields of study in the framework of the mentioned framework can cover a wide range of different issues. In the following, some of the most important fields of study in urban parks will be explained and justified.

**Figure 28.. Recreational-cultural complex of Kerman
revolution**

3.2.5.3 Natural factors

Natural factors of the site include the characteristics of water
resources, geology and soil science, topography, existing
vegetation and micro-climatic conditions of the design area
that should be considered in the design. For example, it should
be noted that in such a case, which has many elevations, the
north-facing parts are noticeably colder and usually shady. It
should also be noted that the climatic conditions of the site are
closely related to the design, planting and selection of plant
species, so that the selection of appropriate species, while
making the necessary arrangements for proper plant growth,
ultimately to make the site climate more favorable. Leads.

3.2.5.4 Artificial agents

The artificial factors of the site can also be summarized in the framework of studying the historical background, social structure and urban context. In designing the park, the effects of their dimensions should be considered. For example, in the mentioned site, the existing physical factors have a historical background and are considered as permanent factors in the design. Even their historical background can be influential in the design, selection of materials and even the creation of new elements. Regarding the social structure, it should be said that the identity of the site should not be formed separately from its social context.

One of the main goals of designing the park is to satisfy Afshar and different age groups of the society and their satisfaction should not be neglected. The situation is the same with the urban context and the formation of the spatial organization and the physical structure of the city should not be considered. View from the inside out, and vice versa to study and design well.

3.2.5.5 Perceptual issues

One's perception of space is directly related to the scales of the elements in space as well as speed. This is such that the space for different viewers at different speeds has multiple effects. When moving at a speed of 70-60 km / h, only large shapes, sharp textures and large masses are seen, and at this speed, small shapes and details of natural artificial elements are not understood. But if the observer is watching these components while walking, he will observe and perceive more details of them. This is very important in designing the edges of the park. For example, in the park in question, the design of the edge next to the main street should be different from the design of the edge next to the local street, as well as the design of the paths inside the park. Therefore, it is necessary to pay attention to it in design. In the park in question, no special attention has been paid to this point, but due to the coincidence of the surfaces located at the edge related to the main street, it conforms to this principle.

3.2.5.6 Security and control agents

Apparently, safety and control aspects are secondary dimensions of park construction projects, because ensuring the security of park spaces and how to control and manage it in practice is beyond the scope of design responsibility. It is true that how the future care and management of the facilities and equipment of a complex after construction and execution is only a figurative aspect and is beyond the scope of project responsibility and how and why it is related to future practical actions and implementation. But at the same time, the pre-determined ideas of the approved plan can provide a favorable ground for providing security and exercising control in the park spaces.

Figure 3.29. Security and control factors of Kerman Revolution entertainment-cultural complex

3.2.5.7 General objectives of the collection
The following objectives should be pursued in the plan:

1- Orientation: The placement of lighting lights in the spaces and paths of the passages can determine their direction and position and guide people in moving towards their desired place.

2- Creating identity: The emphasis of light on turning points or a specific place reveals the identity and its presence and expresses the shape and nature of elements and spaces.

3- Health of people: Lighting lights in different spaces and places should be provided in accordance with their needs and also attention to people's health. Otherwise, the intensity and weakness of the light and the inappropriate height of the pedestals will cause inconvenience to the clients.

4- Creating security: Darkness causes feelings and insecurity in people. The only way to overcome this feeling is to provide the right light in the right place. In addition, one of the ways to deal with destructiveness in parks is to provide adequate lighting.

5- Creating a feature and personality: Light, while expressing the identity of special turning points or spaces, can intensify its feature and in some cases, it expresses different dimensions of this feature.

Therefore, in view of the above, it is worth mentioning that the placement or design of park equipment is a specialized and important work and has its own criteria. Doing these things without studying and using the decision-making method on the spot is considered as unprincipled and primitive work.

3.2.5.8 summary and Conclusion
The city of Kerman, in terms of having tourism talents, is a city with many capabilities that has many opportunities for

development and planning in this field. On the other hand, the municipality, as an urban management organization and also the most important executive body in the city, has many powers to organize and develop these spaces.

Considering these cases, it seems that the most important and first step in organizing and designing recreational spaces, tourism and the like in Kerman, is to prepare a strategic plan for organizing public spaces in this city. In this plan, all the necessary activities are classified according to the recreational and tourist performance in macro and micro scales. After identifying the areas and sub-areas of the city to activate each area, a description of the necessary and appropriate services was prepared and the necessary study areas for intervention in each area are carefully identified. The important point is that the writing of studies and programs to provide specific criteria for urban design in each area is one of the necessities.

Certainly, the use of various experts and efficient consultants will be very effective in providing and promoting the work as well as possible, along with proper supervision by the municipality. This will be the basis for presenting a comprehensive and complete plan that will make the economic, cultural and social prosperity of Kerman for many years to come.

3.2.6 Case study analysis

In this section, based on the table below, the characteristics of the samples studied in this chapter are examined.

row	name	year	country	Scale	Impact of the biophilic approach	Lighting	circulation	Type of plan
1	Bora Bora Hotel	1988	Tahiti located in South Africa	Large scale	The direct impact of nature: the use of nature in the design and construction of houses on the sea and the coastline, the indirect experience of nature: the use of natural materials and natural colors	Coastal	There is a corridor to the assemblies and the beach	Summer houses
2	Lost City Palace		Last City South Africa	Large scale (25 km area)	Creating an artificial natural environment, indirect experience of nature and the use of color, light, natural and indigenous textures	Classic	Complex (with 350 very luxurious rooms, 21 suites)	Lost City Palace
3	Ainak Lake Residential Cultural and Recreation Center		Rasht Iran	Large scale	The use of nature in design, the use of natural elements in construction, and the direct and indirect experience of nature in architecture	Tourist attraction	Use of covered corridors or open joints to connect buildings	Ainak Lake Residential Cultural and Recreation Center
4	Mirza Kuchak Khan Sports and Entertainment Complex		Suleiman Darab neighborhood, Gilan	Approximate area of six hectares	The direct presence of nature in architecture and the use of natural materials, natural light and indigenous colors	Tourist attraction	Logical relationship with peripheral functions	Mirza Kuchak Khan Sports and Entertainment Complex
5	Recreational-cultural complex of Kerman revolution		Kerman	An area of about 4.5 hectares	Use of natural topography and direct presence of nature in design Use of natural colors, natural light and indirect experience of nature in architecture	Tourist attraction	Make connections between functions	Recreational-cultural complex of Kerman revolution

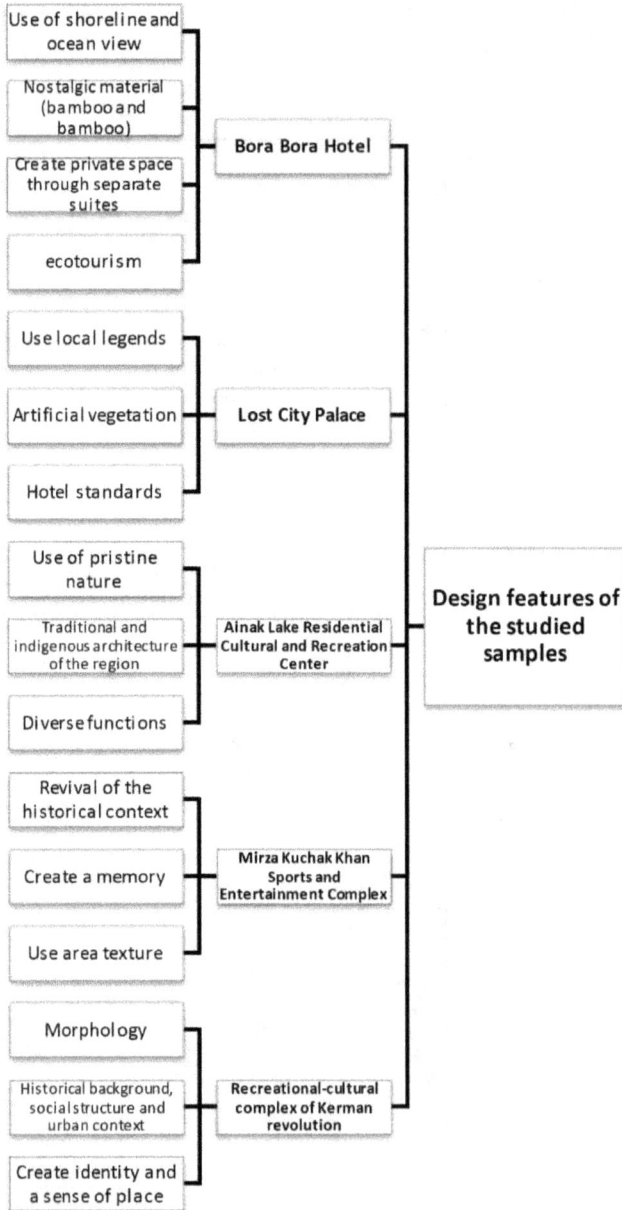

Figure 3.30. Design features of the studied samples

Table 3.2. Factor, criteria and sub-criteria of research.

Factor	Criteria	Subcriteria
Biophilic architecture	Calling nature	Using nature inside the building
		Utilizing nature outside the building
		Green space development
	Physical and mental health	Interior quality
		Outdoor quality
		provide security
	Creativity, attention and learning in children	Create change and movement in the indoor environment
		Create change and movement in the outdoor environment
		Combining building and nature
	Satisfaction with the environment	Creating the desired quality of the interior of the building
		Creating the desired quality outside the building
		Create a favorable landscape
	Productivity and creativity	Increase communication with the natural environment
		Using natural elements
		Evolutionary physical environment
	Neighborhood, interaction and commuting in cities	Spatial hierarchy
		Balance of population density
		Optimal environmental access
	Creates peace of mind and reduces stress	Balance the environment with human auditory, tactile, olfactory and taste stimuli
		Dynamic space and readable routing
		Cultural and ecological relationship with the environment
	Appreciate and understand the value and importance of nature	Use of natural components in environmental buildings such as animals, plants, water;
		Use of natural materials
		Use forms of logic with nature

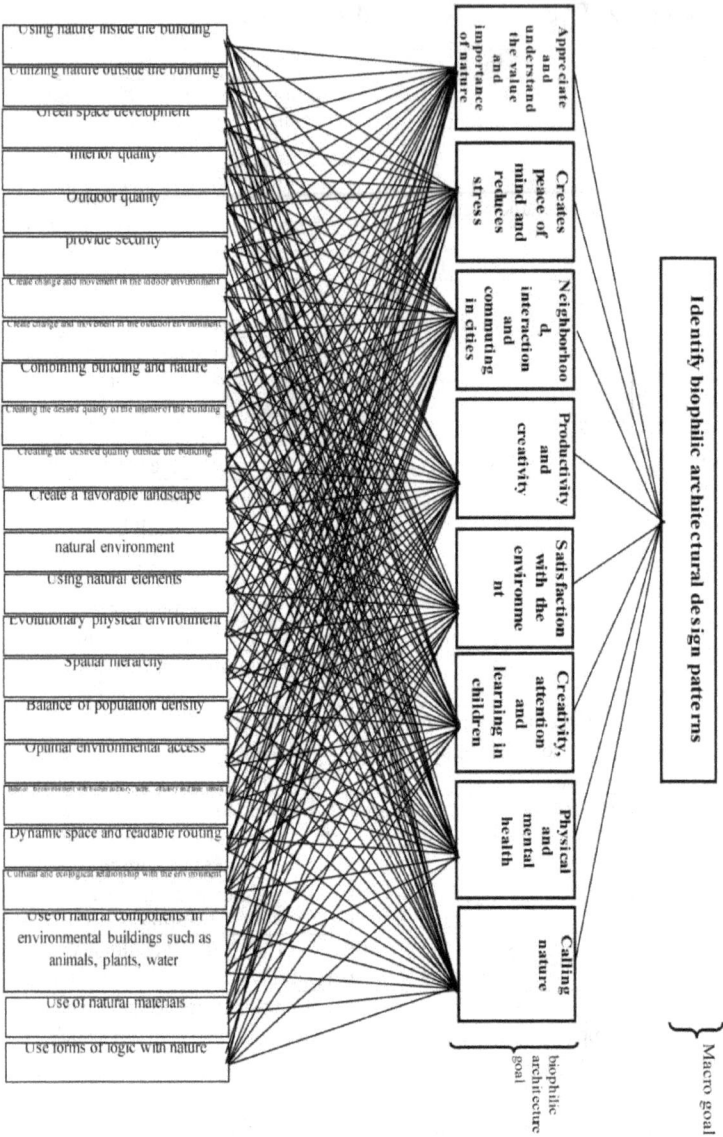

Reference

Affairs, Hojjat and Mehdi Tavakoli Kazeruni, 2018, A Review of Criteria and Standards for Designing Sports Complexes, Second National Conference on Civil Engineering, Architecture with Emphasis on Employment in the Construction Industry, Tehran, Permanent Secretariat of the Conference

Akbari, Siavash (2016). Design of the Museum of Classic Cars with an Approach to Bionic Architecture, Biennial Conference on Society and Contemporary Architecture, Isfahan, Iran.

Bahadori, Mansour (2013) Architecture of aircraft, train, bus and metro stations and terminals.

Cook, J, (1996), Seeking Structure from Nature: The Organic Architecutre of Hungary, Princeton Architectural Press,New Jersey, USA.

Engel, Heino. (2011). Structure Systems, (A. Golsoorat Pahlavani, Trans.), Karang book, Tehran, Iran.

Ernst and Peter Neufert (2013). Newfert Architectural Information, Hossein Mozaffari Tarshizi - Tayebeh Parhizkar, Publisher: Azadeh.

F. V. Vincent, Julian. (2013). Stealing Ideas from Nature, Centre for Biomimetics, The University of Reading, U.K.

Far Kish, Hero; Durrani, Mahsa; Mir Sharghi, Atefeh Sadat (2014). A Study of the Birth Process of Architecture Using Biological Sciences, Ninth Symposium on the Advances of Science and Technology, Mashhad, Iran.

Golabchi, Mahmoud and Morteza Khorsand Nikoo, (2014), Bionic Architecture, University of Tehran Press, Tehran.

Guo, D. (2011). Microstructure and Crystallography of Abalone Shells, University of Glasgow

Hagan, S. (2001), Taking Shape: A New Contract Between Architecture and Nature, Architectural Press, St.Louis,USA.

Haj Esfniari, Mohammad and Masoud Khani Malhem Lou, 2017, The Role of Architecture in Sports Space Design, Third National Conference on Geography and Planning, Modern Architecture and Urban Planning, Qom, Soroush Hekmat Mortazavi Center for Islamic Studies and Research,

Hall, Edward (2008). Hidden dimension, translated by Dr. Manouchehr Tabibian, University of Tehran Press.

Hernandez, C. R. (2006). Thinking Parametric Design: Introducing Parametric Gaudi. Design Studies, (3) 27.

Hernandez, C. R. (2006). Thinking Parametric Design: Introducing Parametric Gaudi. Design Studies, (3)27 http://www.biomimicryinstitute.org

Jackson, A.P. Vincent, J.F.V. Turner, R.M. (1989). A Physical Model of Nacre, Composites Science and Technology,

Jirapong, K. J. Krawczyk, R. (2002). Architectural Forms By Abstracting Nature, Generative Art.

Kalpana S. K. Dinesh R. K. Bedabibhas M. (2010) Biomimetics Learning from Nature ISBN 978-953-307-025.

Karami, Soroush (2011). Redefining the concepts of bionic architecture, a new approach in the field of sustainable architecture, Proceedings of the Second National Conference on Sustainable Architecture, Sama Educational and Cultural Center, Hamadan, Iran.

Kutazadeh, Kiana (2011). A Look at the Air Transport Industry, Bachelor Thesis, Zamani, Ali, Payame Noor University, Central Isfahan, Department of Tourism Management.

Levi, P. (1986), The Periodic Table, (Translated from Italian by Raymond Rosenathal), Abacus Book, London.

Mahmoudinejad, Hadi (2009). Bio-based architecture Specialized publisher of architecture and urban planning.

Mainstone, R. (2001), Developments in Structural Form, Architectural Press; 2nd edition,St.Louis, USA.

Nazarian, Asghar; Qaderi, Ismail; Haghighi, Abdul Reza (2010). Journal of Human Geography - Second Year, Third Issue.

Polano, S. (1996), Santiago Calatrava: Complete Works, Electa, Milan.

Popovic Larsen, O. and Tyas, A. (2003), Conceptual Structural Design, Thomas Telford, London.

Qaruni et al., 2013 Architectural Design with Bionic Approach, A Case Study of Architectural Shells Design with Abalon Oyster, Armanshahr Magazine, 140 Issue 11 Winter 2013-17.

Qaruni, Fatima; Omranipour, Ali; Yazdi, Mohammad (2012). Architectural design with bionic approach, a case study of designing architectural shells inspired by Abalon oyster, Armanshahr architecture and urban planning, No. 11, pp. 140-127.

Rostami, Fatemeh, 2018, New and safe connections and technology inspired by natural elements and systems with bionic approach, the first national welding conference of Borujen Technical and Vocational University, Borujen, Faculty of Engineering and Technology

Sadeghi, Saman, (2007). Bionic Structures and Structures in Shaping Architectural Forms, Online Journal of Civil Engineering Reference (www.civilica.com).

Sadr, Alaleh (2016). Architecture taken from nature, shapes and buildings, 808 Educational and Engineering Institute, specialized in civil and architectural education; (http://www.isca.in/rjrs/archive/v3/i16/3.ISCA-RJRS-322-2013.pdf)

Saffarzadeh, Mahmoud 2000 on Airport Design and Design - Transportation Research Institute Publications, Tehran, Third Edition

Saghaei, Mohsen (2009). Analysis of the Impact of Mehrabad Airport on Economic, Industrial and Tourism Development of Tehran, Journal of Urban and Regional Studies and Research, No. 3, University of Isfahan

Saghaei, Mohsen (2009). Travel and ticket issuance, Isfahan University Jihad Publications.

Salvadori, M. (1990), Why Buildings Stand up, W. W. Norton, London.

Salvadori, Mario G. (1907), Structure in Architecture; the building of buildings, (M. Golabchi,Trans.), Tehran: University of Tehran.

Sanozian, Javier (2010), Biological Process Architecture, translated by Saman Sadeghi, Parham Naghsh Publications, Tehran.

Senusian, Javier (2010). Biological process architecture, translated by Saman Sadeghi, published by Parham Naghsh.

Sharghi, Ali; Ghanbaran, Abdolhamid (2008) Teachings of Nature in Architectural Design, Environmental Science and Technology, No. 1.

Tulayi, Simin (2007). A Review of the Tourism Industry, Tehran, Tarbiat Moallem University, Volume One.

Zahra, qiabkolu (2013). Acoustic design of a multi-purpose conference hall inspired by oyster shell, Journal of Fine Arts - Architecture and Urban Planning, Volume 18, Number 3, pp. 17-24.

Zargham Borujeni, Hamid (2010). Tourism Development Planning, Meh Kameh Publications, Tehran.

www.ingramcontent.com/pod-product-compliance
Lightning Source LLC
Chambersburg PA
CBHW072224270326
41930CB00010B/1988